Because He Said So
(Second Edition)

TAKE JESUS AT HIS WORD

Jeffrey B. Thompson

WestBow
PRESS
A DIVISION OF THOMAS NELSON

Scripture taken from the Holy Bible, New International Version®.
Copyright © 1973, 1978, 1984, 2011 by Biblica, Inc. Used by
permission of Zondervan. All rights reserved worldwide.

WestBow Press books may be ordered through booksellers or by contacting:

WestBow Press
A Division of Thomas Nelson
1663 Liberty Drive
Bloomington, IN 47403
www.westbowpress.com
1-(866) 928-1240

ISBN: 978-1-4497-3740-5 (sc)
ISBN: 978-1-4497-3741-2 (e)

Library of Congress Control Number: 2012901017

Printed in the United States of America

WestBow Press rev. date: 01/23/2012

Contents

Preface

*And the things you have heard me say in the presence
of many witnesses entrust to reliable men who will
also be qualified to teach others.* (2 Timothy 2:2)

We have heard many rules about what God does, when He does
it, why He does it and to whom He will do it. Simple repetition of
these rules through the years may have seemed to make the rules
trustworthy. Error does not become truth by endless repetition.

I ask in reading this book that you take all that you have heard
about salvation, physical healing and mental/emotional healing
and set that aside. I am not asking you to criticize your past
teaching. I am not asking you declare that your prior teaching
was in error in any way. It is not my purpose in this book to
declare erroneous any other teaching on the matters addressed
here. Rather, I intend to emphasize what God's word has to say
on several subjects and relate my experience in relation to each.

I am asking that you, as an exercise of your intellect and will,
examine the ideas set forth in this book without reference to prior
teaching. I ask that you examine the concepts in this book in light
of God's word, and only His word.

When you have finished this book and experienced the power that is available to all who have faith in Jesus, there will be ample time to revisit your prior teaching. With the experience I trust you will have, the understanding of the concepts addressed here and a renewed mind, I then encourage you to re-visit your prior teaching to see what portions of that prior body of knowledge is supported by God's word. Those concepts that originate with the word of God should all align very nicely. Truth stays true throughout eternity.

If you experience an incongruence of your prior concepts and the word of God, I trust you will know which to follow.

The experiences recounted in this book are equally available to all believers. You should expect to participate in miracles, signs and wonders through the renewing of your mind. When you begin to take Jesus at His word, you will find amazing things happening in your home, work, everyday environment and in your church. All of this will happen for only one reason, Because He Said So.

CHAPTER ONE

Be Transformed By Renewing Your Mind

Do not conform any longer to the pattern of this world, but be transformed by the renewing of your mind. Then you will be able to test and approve what God's will is—his good, pleasing and perfect will. (Romans 12:2)

In 2008, my wife, Nancy, and I experienced a major transformation in our lives. Prior to that time, it was common for us to pray for people for salvation, physical healing, emotional and mental healing. We genuinely believed that our prayers made a difference. We saw many instances of change over a period of time. Since 2008, gradual change over a period of time has become the exception rather than the rule.

What happened to us was a renewing of our minds that led to a complete transformation for each of us.

Nancy and I shared a common background. We attended a liturgical church during our "formative" years as followers of Jesus. We were impressed with the importance of sanctification. To be sure, we were clear that Jesus accepts us just as we are. No one taught us that we needed to clean up our act in order to be accepted into eternal life. We clearly understood that faith in Jesus, not works, was the key to salvation.

However, once we had faith in Jesus, we both tended to believe that God would simply be happier with us if we didn't sin so much. At times we applied ourselves to this effort. At times, our effort was "not so much."

I confess to misapprehending Paul's admonition to "be transformed by the renewing of your mind."

As a lawyer I am well trained to examine the literal meaning of words in statutes and cases. My livelihood has required me to analyze just what the language used means. In spite of this training and experience, I understood Paul's admonition backwards.

I believed that if I would transform my behavior, my thinking would be transformed. This was a particularly attractive proposition to me because I always had more trouble with my thoughts than with my actions. I am not suggesting my actions were good. I am confessing that no matter how degenerate and unredeemed my actions may have been, I was always holding back a little. My thought life was the arena of virtually no control. After all, if you don't tell anyone what you are thinking, you can disguise bad thoughts with not too bad actions.

Thus, my reading of Paul's admonition was "clean up your act and your thinking will fall in line." Although I do not recall any preacher ever saying it that way, the sentiment was consistent with my belief that God would love me better if I acted better. Most of the sermons I can recall contained at least a kernel of "clean up your act" in addition to any other idea. All I needed was a suggestion that it was possible for me to clean up my act and I was headed full speed in that direction. What a disappointment to find that I simply could not do it.

I may even have believed that Jesus came to enable me to have the will and ability to clean up my act. I am certain no preacher ever said that, but it just kind of snuck into the recesses of my mind.

It now seems ludicrous to me that I would believe that I had any ability to clean up my act. Surely if it was possible for me to do that, Jesus didn't need to come and endure death on the cross for me. How silly of Him to offer the ultimate sacrifice if I had the ability within me! I am frankly embarrassed at even the possibility that I believed that I had or would be able to attain the ability to conform my behavior to the requirements of the Law.

Change Your Way of Thinking

Jesus was very clear that we need to change the way we think. The Gospel of Mark gets right to it.

> *After John was put in prison, Jesus went into Galilee, proclaiming the good news of God. "The time has come," He said. "The kingdom of God is near. Repent and believe the good news!"* (Mark 1:14-15)

Jesus proclaimed the "good news." Maybe you have heard the "good news" restricted to the promise that we are saved (from hell) by grace through faith in Jesus, a very limited message. "You can change your ultimate destination from hell to heaven."

Salvation results from receiving Jesus' invitation to indwell you with His Holy Spirit when you ask Him to be Lord and Savior of your life. Are you "all over" the "Savior" part (change in destination) but not so fond of the "Lord" part? Do you view salvation as a form of fire insurance? Fire insurance is good—I am just not convinced that fire insurance is available as a stand-alone product.

What about life insurance? Jesus said He came to give us an abundant life. (John 10:10) The life available to us comes from the indwelling of the Holy Spirit. This indwelling brings far more than fire insurance!

Jesus was reporting the "good news." *"The time has come."* Jesus was on the scene changing everything. There was no delay, no need to wait. *"The time has come."* Time for what? It was time for Jesus to make available a completely new reality, entrance into the kingdom of God.

"The kingdom of God is near." The good news Jesus was urging us to believe is that the good news of the kingdom of God was replacing the Law and the Prophets. The Law served the purpose of demonstrating to us that no one was capable of compliance. We need a Savior! The Prophets served the purpose of advising us of the identity of the Savior (Messiah) and what he would be like. Jesus said the Law and the Prophets were until John (the Baptist). Since then, there is a new sheriff in town. (Luke 16:16; Matthew 11:12-13)

Jesus said, *"Repent and believe the good news!"* Repent is usually understood as a verb dealing with both feeling sorry (perhaps even ashamed) of both thoughts and actions and changing my behavior to clean up my flesh. *Repent* is broader than that.

Repent deals with Godly sorrow, not worldly sorrow. The concept of Godly sorrow is vastly different from the concept of worldly sorrow.

> *"Godly sorrow brings repentance that leads to salvation and leaves no regret, but worldly sorrow brings death."* (2 Corinthians 7:10)

Properly understood, repentance wears a smiley face. Worldly sorrow does not bring repentance. Rather, worldly sorrow brings death. Repentance does not bring Godly sorrow. Rather, Godly sorrow brings repentance. The fruit of repentance is salvation with no regret. In true repentance, there is no lingering sense of shame and sorrow for the past.

Repent, in this passage, comes from the Greek word (the original language of the New Testament) *metanoia* which means to change your way of ***thinking***, not ***acting***. A change in your way of thinking may well, and probably should, change your actions. We have a "chicken and egg" problem here. What comes first? Trying to change my actions has not changed my thinking. A change in my thinking has dramatically changed my actions.

Look at Jesus' command again. *"Repent and believe the good news!"* This command is a single sentence. He didn't say repent only. He didn't say believe the good news only. He tied both of those together. We are to repent *and* believe the good news. In this context it is clear that Jesus is commanding a change of attitude and attention. He is commanding us to change the latitude of our attitude. Jesus' command, paying careful heed to the Greek language, is:

> Change your way of thinking and believe the good news.

When are we to change our way of thinking? Jesus said the time is now. When are we to believe the good news? Jesus said the time is now.

What is the good news? The kingdom of God is near. Jesus brought his reality with Him. Jesus was making entry into the kingdom available. Entry into the kingdom should bring with it a change in thinking. In the kingdom, the emphasis is no longer on the Law and the Prophets but on kingdom realities.

Nancy and I changed our way of thinking in 2008. I cannot adequately express how exciting it has been to be *"transformed by the renewing of our minds."* Paul tells us that the result of the renewing of our minds is that we will "*be able to test and approve what God's will is—His good, pleasing and perfect will.*" (Romans 12:2) We see His will demonstrated all the time.

We no longer believe that we pray for others to change God's mind. Rather, we believe that we have learned His good and perfect will in relation to salvation, healing and delivery from torment. Jesus healed all who were afflicted by the devil. (Acts 10:38) God's mind is already made up—no need for a change.

Take Jesus at His Word

Prior to 2008 I read around the largest and best promises in the Bible. I read the promises. I prayed for others. The results I prayed for did not appear to have happened in most instances. This disappointment gave birth to imaginations and denials of the truth of the Word. Oh, I knew the Word was true; it was just truer for others than it was for me.

Nancy and I feel that we almost stepped into a parallel universe in 2008 and have stayed there ever since because our minds continue to be renewed. We began to participate in miracles, signs and wonders at an ever increasing rate. Now, we expect that God will miraculously intervene on a regular basis. Miraculous healings seems to be the rule rather than the exception. It is our usual experience to see God deliver His compassion to His people by miraculous healings and delivery from torment.

As our minds were becoming renewed, we began to take Jesus at His word. The Gospel of John contains an account of a man who took Jesus at His word. God changed his history as a result.

While Jesus was in Cana, he was approached by a royal official who had a son in Capernaum, sick and close to death. (John 4:46-54) This official was not a member of any tribe of Israel but rather was most likely an official in Herod's court in Capernaum.

Even though he was not a Jew, he had heard about Jesus, perhaps through the reports of Jesus' turning the water into wine at the wedding feast in Cana.

When Jesus returned to Cana for the first time after this wedding miracle, the royal official went to Jesus and begged Him to come to his home and heal his son. The official showed either a lot of faith in Jesus or the desperation of his situation when he sought out a Jew for healing. He would have known that, according to Jewish law, Jesus would have little, if anything, to do with a Gentile. He certainly would not be expected to visit the home of a Gentile, regardless of the reason. The royal official was asking Jesus to violate the law by associating with him and going to his home to heal his son.

Jesus seems to have mildly rebuked the official, saying *"Unless you people see miraculous signs and wonders, you will never believe."* (John 4:48) It is not clear whether Jesus was specifically addressing the official or a crowd of Galileans. Perhaps he was referring to the lack of faith He had noticed in his home town. (Matthew 13:58) In any event, it is clear that the official already believed. He sought out Jesus and begged Him to come to his home in Capernaum to heal his son.

If the rebuke was directed at the official, he was undeterred. He said, *"Sir, come down before my child dies."* (John 4:49)

Jesus did not directly refuse to go to the official's home, but said, *"You may go. Your son will live."* (John 4:50) Jesus dismissed the official with a promise his son would live. There is no report that Jesus laid hands on the official who was standing in the gap for his son. There is no report that Jesus prayed for the son's healing. The sole report is that He promised the official that his son would live.

The official's response to this promise was extraordinary. He did not plead and beg Jesus to come and heal his son in the same manner He had healed others. Because Jesus offered no touch, no prayer, no word of encouragement, no exhortation to the son to recover, and did not command any evil spirit to come out of the son, the official could have been easily excused if he had tried to convince Jesus his son was worthy of healing and a little effort. I would have insisted that Jesus at least come into my son's presence and *do something*. It would be understandable if the official had asked Jesus for an anointed prescription or specific instructions of what the son should do to regain his health.

The official did none of those things. Rather, the official "took Jesus at his word and departed." (John 4:50) Now, that is a demonstration of complete faith in Jesus. In essence he said, "Jesus said it. I believe it. That settles it."

He was not going home to heal his son. He was going home because Jesus had *promised* that there was nothing more required. It was done when Jesus said, "your son will live." God's word had completed its purpose when Jesus said it. The royal official knew his son would live Because He Said So.

While he was still on his way home, the official learned that his son was living. He didn't ask how his son started on the road to recovery. He didn't ask whether anyone at his home had taken any heroic steps. He didn't ask about any prayers for healing. He simply asked **when** the healing manifested in his son's body.

When he learned that the fever had left the boy at the same time that Jesus promised his recovery, he reported that occurrence to his household. The result was that "*he and all his household believed.*" (John 4:53) The report of what Jesus had done, the testimony of Jesus, changed the atmosphere in the official's household and all believed.

With the renewing of our minds in 2008, we changed our way of thinking. Now, we do the best we can to take Jesus at His word in order to believe:

o   Jesus was manifested to destroy the works of the devil (1 John 3:8);

o   Jesus' atoning sacrifice was completely sufficient for forgiveness of sin, physical healing and delivery from torment (Isaiah 53:4-5);

o   God anointed Jesus of Nazareth with the Holy Spirit and with power (Acts 10:38);

o   Jesus went around doing good, healing all who were oppressed by the devil, because God was with Him (Acts 10:38);

o   Jesus acted in the power of the Holy Spirit because He could do only what He saw his Father do (John 5:19);

o   Jesus spoke in the power of the Holy Spirit because He said only what He heard the Father say (John 8:28; John 12:50);

o   Whoever hears Jesus' word and believes Him who sent Jesus has eternal life and will not be condemned; he has crossed over from death to life (John 5:24);

o   Jesus sent us just as the Father had sent Him (John 20:21);

o   We have received power from on high in the baptism of the Holy Spirit (Luke 24:49; Acts 1:4-8);

o   Anyone who has faith in Jesus will do what He did, and even greater things than these, because Jesus went to the Father (John 14:12); and

o   Jesus will do whatever we ask in His name, so that the Son may bring glory to the Father; we may ask Him for anything in His name, and He will do it (John 14:13).

No longer do we read these promises out of scripture. No longer do we read around these promises, supposing they are for others but not for us. Rather, we take Jesus at His word. As a result, everything has changed!

God Heals Through Doctors
And Words of Others

Before 2008, we recognized that God heals miraculously through the words of others and through individuals in the healing professions. Many times we were certain that God's hand was all over a particular circumstance bringing recovery to health to a person in dire need.

Nancy and I moved to Ruidoso New Mexico in 1999 for me to die. By the time we moved to Ruidoso, I was taking 12 prescription medications each day and was on a first name basis with the pharmacy staff at Walgreens.

When we got settled in Ruidoso, we found that our good friends, Ron and Doris Thomson (they never have learned how to spell their last name correctly) had relocated there following his retirement as an Episcopal priest in El Paso. After renewing our friendship, we began seeing them socially on a very occasional basis.

One of the hallmarks of my disability is that my short-term memory was significantly compromised. During this period of disability, Nancy and I went to Ron's and Doris' house for an evening playing bridge. I was unable to finish most sentences during our evening of conversation. Nancy had already become very adept at discerning what story I was trying to tell, what feeling I was trying to convey, or the question I was trying to ask. She finished the job when I got stuck, which was most of the time.

At the end of the evening, it was clear that Doris had become increasingly alarmed through the evening with my inability to function in casual conversation. I have no recollection of what that conversation was, but I have a very clear recollection of watching her eyes get wider and wider through the night.

At the end of the evening, while we were making our way to the front door, she asked me, "Jeff, do you want to get well?"

I recognized the question from the account in the Gospel of John when Jesus healed the crippled man at the pool of Bethesda. (John 5:1-8) When Jesus asked whether that man wanted to get well, the man offered a host of explanations why the healing that was available when the angel troubled the waters in the pool of Bethesda was not available to him.

When Doris asked, I took some time to decide whether I, indeed, wanted to get well. The man lying daily beside the pool of Bethesda did not need to get well. His basic needs were met each day. Apparently he ate regularly and did not need to work. All he had to do was tolerate his condition.

I was not experiencing great difficulty tolerating my condition. I received a regular, tax-free check each month from my disability insurance company. We had no mortgage on our house. I was cared for by my wife in a very loving, kind, gentle manner. No one made any claims on my time to help them solve their problems. Basically, I had no pressure on me to perform in any respect. And best of all, each day's aches and pains appeared to be brand-new that day.

So, what would it mean if I got well? Would I only get well enough to have a more complete understanding of my circumstances? Would I only get well enough to permit me to work as a lawyer with an adequate memory while still having the aches, pains and breathing problems I was experiencing? Just what would it mean to get well?

I had already decided, and Nancy and I had discussed, that we knew where we are going when our physical bodies die. Since I felt I had an assurance of heaven and that Nancy would be there,

I felt no urgency to hold on to this life. To the extent I understood this life, it was fraught with difficulties. To the extent I did not understand this life, Nancy was handling that.

In relatively short order, I decided that my answer to Doris' question was "yes," although it was not an enthusiastic "yes."

With my consent, Nancy, Ron and Doris prayed for my recovery. I had no real expectation of improvement.

The next weeks, months and years were quite amazing. It was obvious to Nancy and me that God's hand was all over what was happening and that it began with Doris' question, "Do you want to get well?"

o The short story of what happened next includes: my disability insurance company informed me that it was terminating my benefits because it had determined that I had recovered and, furthermore, had never been sick.

o I sought treatment from a Doctor of Oriental Medicine (DOM) for treatment of tendinitis in both of my elbows who diagnosed a complete shut-down of my immune system in 1993.

o Nancy and I traveled to Austin where I again sought treatment for tendinitis from an acupuncturist-chiropractor-kinesiologist who had a strong background in diet and nutrition who recommended testing which showed I had a significant problem with Candida Albicans, a naturally occurring yeast in the gut.

o A medical doctor prescribed an anti-fungal medication to treat the yeast problem.

o Upon re-occurrence of all of my symptoms, I was referred by the DOM to a doctor of naturopathy (ND).

On the way home an appointment with the ND, Nancy and I had a meeting in our car. We were lamenting the fact that the DOM had one protocol, the MD had another and the ND had still a third. We respected each of these individuals.

I told Nancy, "it is obvious to me we must make a choice about which doctor will become the 'go to guy.' We were in agreement that the ND was clearly the class act so we chose her. Within three years I recovered excellent brain function with no noticeable memory impairment, and a robustness of my immune system which I was convinced was gone forever.

We have no question that God intervened in the person of Doris Thomson with that biblical question, "Do you want to get well?" When we explained to her the significance we attributed to that question, she said, "I never asked that question before. I don't know why I asked it then."

My recovery was anything but instantaneous. However, Nancy and I are convinced that what happened was just as much a miracle as if it had happened that way. The entire experience reinforced our long-held belief that God is continually guiding and directing our paths. He places those we need in our midst for our benefit. We have no question that God heals through doctors, all kinds of doctors.

Instantaneous Healing—But Why?

We also have experienced instantaneous healings. Both Nancy and I have been healed at least four times each in quite different ways. However, in each instance it was clear that God had intervened in our lives.

In 2004 I was diagnosed as having a preliminary stage of melanoma on my right leg just below my knee. The initial biopsy was quick and simple. Ten days later I received a call from the doctor who said, "Jeff, the biopsy showed a very preliminary stage of melanoma. Now melanoma is not like basal cell carcinoma. In its advanced stages we advise patients to not buy season tickets to anything. I simply need to cut out the melanoma until the 'margins are clear' and that will be the end of it."

For sixteen days after the first biopsy, the biopsy site was an open, running sore with a bright red circle of infection surrounding the site. The Sunday before I was scheduled to return to Austin for the procedure, I asked for prayer at First Baptist Church in Ruidoso for my "condition."

I was conflicted about whether I should ask for prayer. After all, I knew that God's intervention was not really necessary. The doctor was already on the case. A simple procedure would produce a complete cure. Why bother God with his one?

About twenty-five people gathered around me in the middle of the service. I did not really expect to see any immediate change in my leg.

When I went home after church I changed out of my long pants into shorts. I immediately noticed that the biopsy site was completely scabbed over and the redness was completely gone.

Nancy and I discussed whether to proceed with the planned procedure. We were both certain I had been completely healed. We decided we would proceed to "testify to the doctor."

We made it to the dermatologist on Wednesday next. During the procedure the doctor removed a substantial plug flesh from my leg which required about fifteen stitches to close. I never felt any pain after the original local anesthetic was injected. I had no discomfort until the stitches were removed.

Ten days after the procedure, the dermatologist called with the pathology results. He said, "Good news, the margins are clear."

I asked, "Yes, but tell me, was there any melanoma in the sample?"

"Well, no." He responded

For months after this experience I asked everyone who would listen, "Why does God heal people? Is it for the person healed or the people who see the healing?"

The most knowledgeable people responded simply, "Yes."

I did not **need** God to heal me. The medical knowledge was well developed and the procedure was scheduled. Why then did God bother to heal me miraculously?

He healed me miraculously because that is who He is. Healing is part of God's DNA.

A New Question

Nearly four years later, a new question occurred to me. Do you think we see fewer miracles than we would like to see just because we don't ask often enough? The question in another context could be stated, "Do you think we don't catch as many fish as we would like simply because we don't keep our lure in the water?

A seasoned fisherman will tell you that catching more fish requires having your lure in the water. The fish don't jump in the boat. But, that same fisherman will tell you it makes a difference where you fish, when you fish, what lure you use and how you present the lure.

Nancy and I started voraciously pursuing all we could find about divine healing. Were miracles, signs and wonders only occasional occurrences which could be neither predicted nor expected? Or, did miracles, signs and wonders likewise depend upon where, when, and how?

We were shaken to our core when we listened to a 6-CD teaching by Bill Johnson, the senior pastor of Bethel Church in Redding, California entitled *Healing, Our Neglected Birthright*. The reports in that CD series of multiple miraculous interventions of God were, frankly, unbelievable. As we listened to this series repeatedly, our acceptance of the truth of these reports increased.

We learned that Bill Johnson was speaking at Sojourn Church in Carrollton, Texas, about 75 miles from our home. We decided to go. I was quite interested to see if anyone would be healed "on purpose." If anyone was healed on purpose, I wanted to hear the prayers and see the process. What could we learn about where, when and how?

We not only saw people healed on purpose, we both experienced it ourselves. One of the principles we learned from Bill Johnson is that prayer need not be a long, drawn out process. Short prayers work.

Nancy had already had nine surgeries on her hands and wrist for arthritis related problems. She had a particular problem with the PIP joint in her fingers and not much of a problem in the rest of her hands. She had already had multiple surgeries to place plastic spacers in the PIP joint of several of her fingers. Over a short time, several of those spacers "failed."

Ultimately she received carbon steel joints in four of her fingers. Her surgeries gave her a significant reduction in pain but her function was quite limited. I was becoming acquainted with running a vacuum cleaner and making the bed. Although Nancy had always been a happy cooker and quite accomplished in the kitchen, her gradual loss of dexterity had severely limited her capabilities.

To our great surprise, Bill Johnson announced that they had been seeing great results of healings for people with artificial joints. He asked those with artificial joints to raise their hands.

Since I have an artificial left shoulder and Nancy has her many artificial PIP joints, we both had our hands raised. Surely Bill would be inviting those with their hands raised to the front so that he could pray for them. In the alternative, maybe some "professional prayers" had come with him who would pray for us. I wanted to hear those prayers.

Much to our collective surprise, neither Bill Johnson nor any professionals even offered to pray. Instead, he invited those in the audience surrounding those with raised hands to gather around them and "give them your best prayer." It seemed like we needed more instruction than that.

The man who offered to pray for Nancy offered a shocking prayer for her hands. His "best prayer" consisted, in its entirety, of "Well, God, heal her hands." Casper Milquetoast could have done better.

Bill Johnson then instructed those who had received prayer to "check it out. Do something you couldn't do before."

Nancy checked her flexibility and found no change. She was pretty sure that "Casper" simply had failed her.

Bill Johnson then instructed those who had not yet been healed to seek prayer once again. The only person available to Nancy was good old "Casper." Maybe this time he would have a more powerful prayer.

"Casper" didn't improve at all. He seemed to have this particular prayer memorized, "Well, God, heal her hands."

Over the next twenty four hours, Nancy realized that the flexibility in her hands gradually improved. By the time we attended the next evening session, she was able to make a fist with each hand without pain, something that she had not been able to do for several years.

Her flexibility and dexterity continued to improve and I can report that not only can she peel fruit and manipulate kitchen utensils better than she had been able to for ten years, I am no longer called upon to make the bed or run the vacuum cleaner. **Alleluia**!

Oh yes, my shoulder. I raised my hand. Two men came and prayed for me some of the most beautiful prayers I had ever heard, on two occasions. Their prayers were real confidence builders but *nothing happened.*

I did mention that I was likewise healed. It didn't involve my shoulder. While I was praying for a man with scoliosis in his back the next night we finished early. I started to return to my chair and he said "What about you?"

I had a significant problem with my back prompted in large part by cutting about 200 trees with a chain saw on our property in Ruidoso. It had now been about three years since the original abuse and my back was really sore.

I said, "I have a sore back."

He said, "Well, let's pray for it."

He and another man standing behind me prayed a quick prayer for my back. We didn't have much time since Bill Johnson allows about 90 seconds for the prayer and we had already prayed for the scoliosis.

I thanked the man and returned to my seat. When I got out of bed the following morning, I realized that the pain in my back was significantly improved. My condition continued to improve over time.

With a quick count at the end of the conference, 184 people professed to having been healed during the conference. The most "significant" was probably a woman who had sight restored in one eye. The most "important" for us was Nancy's hands.

God does heal His people "on purpose." We were now hooked and needed to know everything we could learn about this process.

Praying, reading, re-reading, listening and re-listening kept us totally on fire about miracles, signs and wonders. The breakthrough we experienced came as a result of the renewing of our minds.

We did not renew our minds. God did. The renewing of your mind comes through revelation knowledge. While you cannot learn it, voracious pursuit of Jesus opens your mind to things you have been aware of yet completely missed in the past.

We listened innumerable times to the 6-CD series on *Healing, Out Neglected Birthright*. Each time we heard phrases in a new light. We sought out the referenced scriptures and reviewed them in many translations. How had we missed all this information?

We read about the people in past ages who experienced significant healing ministries. Much to our surprise, the concepts Bill Johnson explained so well were well known and taught from the middle of the 1800's. Where had it all gone? How had we missed these truths?

Perhaps, like me, you have paid no attention to Jesus' promise:

> *Any who has faith in me will do what I have been doing. He will do even greater things than these, because I am going to my Father.* (John 14:12)

To be sure, I knew that promise was in my Bible. To be equally sure, I knew it had nothing to do with me. I am very happy to report that I was wrong! We now fully expect to do the things Jesus did.

Nancy and I now understand that God heals His people because He loves them. He has already paid the price for the healing. The healing is a "done deal" in the kingdom.

God does not miraculously intervene only when there is no other way out! When your mind has been renewed, you are on the path to seeing God heal His people "on purpose."

CHAPTER TWO

The Key Which Unlocks the Door

I keep asking that the God of our Lord Jesus Christ, the glorious Father, may give you the Spirit of wisdom and revelation, so that you may know him better. I pray also that the eyes of your heart may be enlightened in order that you may know the hope to which he has called you, the riches of his glorious inheritance in the saints, and his incomparably great power for us who believe. That power is like the working of his mighty strength, which he exerted in Christ when he raised him from the dead and seated him at his right hand in the heavenly realms, far above all rule and authority, power and dominion, and every title that can be given, not only in the present age but also in the one to come. (Ephesians 1:17-21)

The natural mind is not prepared to comprehend spiritual truths. *The man without the Spirit does not accept the things that come from the Spirit of God, for they are foolishness to him, and he cannot understand them, because they are spiritually discerned.* (1 Corinthians 2:14) After teaching this material many times, Nancy and I have learned that acceptance of this teaching requires an equipping by God.

Paul prayed for the Ephesians that God would give them three things: hope, riches and incomparably great power. He described that power as the same power that God exerted when He raised Jesus from the dead. If the Ephesians needed those three things, perhaps it would be wise if we did our best to obtain all three and in the same way. Just like Paul, we need to ask God for them.

If we are to change our way of thinking and be renewed by the transforming of our mind, clearly we need help. Is that help available? You bet.

After healing the paralytic beside the Pool of Bethesda, Jesus was beset by the Jews who were determined to kill him. These particular Jews were well versed in the scriptures but did not recognize Jesus. More than that, they did not recognize that Jesus was healing through the power of God.

Jesus told them,

> *You diligently study the Scriptures because you think that by them you possess eternal life. These are the Scriptures that testify about me, yet you refuse to come to me to have life.* (John 5:39)

Although they observed Jesus directly, they placed their reliance solely upon the written word. Even though the Prophets clearly pointed to Jesus, these Jews missed Him and rejected Him as the Messiah.

We need to come to Jesus to possess eternal life, and all that is included with it. Reading the scriptures without coming to Jesus leaves us incomplete.

Each of the four Gospels record John the Baptist identifying Jesus as the one who would baptize with the Holy Spirit. If this baptism were not important, it would not be in each of the Gospels.

The Holy Spirit makes some believers nervous. This unfamiliarity arises from bad teaching and lack of experience. It is helpful to recall that the Holy Spirit is none other than God Himself. He is no scarier than Jesus or God the Father. He just hasn't been discussed positively in some polite circles. Nonetheless, He is an old friend who is always on our side and up to nothing but good for each of us.

It makes no sense whatsoever to say, "I believe in God the Father and Jesus, His one and only Son but I am not so sure about that Holy Spirit guy. He scares me." The Holy Spirit is a person, not an unknown force that is somewhat out of control.

The Holy Spirit has not "retired." He did not become tired at the end of the Apostolic Age and check into heaven's Old Folks Home. He is active in the world today as He resides in us.

The Holy Spirit who resides in me is the same Holy Spirit who worked through Jesus. Believers receive life by the indwelling of the Holy Spirit at the time of salvation. It is His life that Jesus imparts to us when we *cross over from death to life.*" (John 5:24) He is *in* all believers. The Holy Spirit is *in* us for our benefit.

Just as Jesus received power at His baptism with the Holy Spirit at the time of His baptism by John, The Holy Spirit is *upon us* after our baptism with the Holy Spirit. He is *upon us* for the benefit of others.

The Holy Spirit who is *upon* us has all the same power He had when He was *upon* Jesus. We do not receive Holy Spirit, Jr. We do not receive Holy Spirit, Lite. The indwelling power of the Holy Spirit includes the fullness of the power of God. I may not be strong. He is omnipotent.

Spiritual Gifts and Manifestations

Paul explained spiritual gifts to the church at Corinth.

> *Now about spiritual gifts, brothers, I do not want you to be ignorant . . . . There are different kinds of gifts, but the same Spirit. There are different kinds of service, but the same Lord. There are different kinds of working, but the same God works all of them in all men. Now to each one the manifestation of the Spirit is given for the common good.* (1 Corinthians 12:1-7)

Each spiritual gift is a manifestation of the Holy Spirit, given for the common good. The Greek word translated "manifestation" is *phanerosis* which means an exhibition or expression. The root word in Greek is *phaneroo* which means to render apparent or show oneself. Although all believers are indwelt by the Holy Spirit, there may be no manifestation of the Holy Spirit in their lives. That is, the Holy Spirit is *in* them but not *upon* them.

Baptism in the Holy Spirit puts a sure and certain *phanerosis* within reach of every believer. Paul tells us that a manifestation of the Spirit is given to each of us. The manifestation is not given for our amusement. Rather, the manifestation is given for the common good. If a gift does not serve the common good, it is not a *phanerosis* of the Holy Spirit. Unless the outflow in my life is directed to the common good, the outflow is not a manifestation of the Holy Spirit.

Peter reminded the Gentile Cornelius that after Jesus was anointed by God with the Holy Spirit and with power He went around doing good. (Acts 10:38) The Greek word translated "good" means a philanthropic act. When Jesus was "doing good" He was letting the Holy Spirit flow through Him, not performing morally upright acts. A philanthropist is one who gives away his treasure. That is exactly what Jesus was doing, giving away the treasure of the kingdom. That is exactly what we are called to do.

I am not suggesting Jesus' acts were not morally upright. Rather, I am suggesting that moral rectitude was not the hallmark of the "good" that Jesus was doing. He gave away all that the Holy Spirit had given Him by doing what He saw the Father do and saying only what He heard the Father say. All of this power was directed toward destroying the works of the devil. (1 John 3:8)

Paul makes it clear that the different gifts, the different service and the different works are all the product of the same God working in men. In each instance, it is God working, not man.

Paul then proceeds to list nine gifts of the Holy Spirit.

o   Word of wisdom;
o   Word of knowledge;
o   Faith;
o   Gifts of healing;
o   Miraculous powers;
o   Prophecy;
o   Distinguishing between spirits;
o   Speaking in different tongues; and
o   Interpretation of tongues.

The renewing of your mind and the ability to take Jesus at His Word requires a boost in your faith. How convenient that Faith is one of the spiritual gifts. If you are thirsting for the Faith to enable your mind to be renewed and to take Jesus at His Word, you may simply ask Jesus for that particular gift when you ask for Baptism in the Holy Spirit.

All of these gifts "are the work of one and the same Spirit." (1 Corinthians 12:11) Since God is always working, manifestations of the Holy Spirit are always available. (John 5:17) When the

Body of Christ is assembled, these manifestations of the Holy Spirit are distributed among the Body as God determines. We do not determine through whom the manifestation will be given. We don't always know through whom God will choose to act at any occasion.

When I was baptized with the Holy Spirit in the late 1970's I became increasingly aware of manifestations of the Holy Spirit in my life. My faith simply sky-rocketed and the increase seemed unrelated to anything I had done or was doing. I just knew that there was a new-found confidence in my relationship with God and His benevolent attitude toward me.

Words of knowledge, words of wisdom and discerning between spirits were somewhat surprising gifts because they appeared with no rational basis and no relation to particular circumstances which might be interpreted to have given rise to a thought or idea. Instead, all of a sudden, the idea or knowledge was available, fully formed. It didn't require any further input from me.

I learned early on that I could not increase the occurrence of these gifts nor demand that I know things for my sole benefit. I might receive some direction for my life as an answer to prayer but true words of knowledge and wisdom appeared irrespective of my will and outside my control.

In relation to tongues, I understood that unless the Holy Spirit was speaking, there would be no utterance in tongues. I also knew that unless I provided my tongue, nothing would be forced from my mouth.

My experience with knowledge, wisdom, tongues and discerning between spirits did not prepare me to properly apprehend the gifts of healing or miraculous powers. When it came to gifts of healing and miraculous powers, I believed that if I had either of those gifts, I would know it and be changed by it. I expected one who had the gifts of healing to feel empowered in a personal sense. I further expected that one with the gifts of healing would be able to bring healings into existence by the power given him.

It doesn't make sense that I could fully understand that I could not "gin up" a word of knowledge or a word of wisdom but still believed that one who had received a gift of healing would be able to produce healing upon demand. I knew I didn't feel empowered in relation to knowledge and wisdom. It simply came when it came. Why in the world, then, would I have a different expectation when it came to a gift of healing?

When I am confused, it helps to go back to the Owner's Manual, the Bible. Since all spiritual gifts are manifestations of the Holy Spirit, it is always the Holy Spirit who is acting, not the individual. I could easily accept that I could not "know" the unlearned and unlearnable. Rather, the Holy Spirit knew and would share that knowledge with me for the benefit of others. Somehow I was confused about healing. I just didn't see it as simple as it is. All healings, all miracles, all signs and all wonders are done directly by God and God alone and are manifestations of His presence here with us. God manifests Himself among us for His glory, not for ours.

I was helped significantly in my limited understanding of this gift of healing when I read an article by A. B. Simpson (1843-1919). Simpson was the founder of the Christian and Missionary Alliance and wrote more than seventy books on the Bible and the Christian way of life. In an article entitled *"Himself"* A. B. Simpson wrote:

> *I often hear people say, 'I wish I could get hold of Divine Healing, but I cannot.' Sometimes they say, 'I have got it.' If I ask them, 'What have you got?' the answer is sometimes, I've got the blessing; I have got*

the theory; I have got the healing; and sometimes I have got the sanctification.

But I thank God that we have been taught that it is not the blessing, it is not the healing, it is not the sanctification, it is not the thing, it is not the it that you want, but it is something better. It is 'the Christ'; it is Himself . . . .

It is the person of Jesus Christ we want.

At last He said to me—Oh so tenderly—'My child, just take Me, and let Me be in you the constant supply of all this, Myself.'

Jesus explained that by Himself He could do nothing. (John 5:19) He was careful to say only what He heard the Father saying and to say it just as He was instructed. (John 12:49) He waited for the power of the Lord to be present to heal. (Luke 5:17)

Even after God anointed Jesus of Nazareth with the Holy Spirit and with power, he could do nothing by Himself, He said nothing on His own accord, and He didn't have the power to heal. He relied totally upon the power of the Holy Spirit to manifest the presence and power of God. He awaited the *phanerosis* of the Holy Spirit.

When we realize that the healing power resides in Jesus, Himself, and that we have nothing in us to add, the pressure for healing and miraculous signs evaporates. If Jesus does the healing, the person gets healed. If Jesus does not heal, there is no healing. It certainly is not going to come from me.

The Purpose of Signs

Signs provide a direction to a greater reality than the sign itself. I cannot exit through an exit sign. Rather, I use the exit sign to find the location of the exit door. If a sign doesn't point the way to a greater reality, it is useless. There is no purpose in the zing and the zang of signs unless the zing and the zang point to God's presence and power. Miracles, signs and wonders will never point to a human being. They only point to Jesus, Himself.

It's Not Me

The full panoply of spiritual gifts may well not be known to man. I am certain that the spiritual gifts we know about which manifest the Holy Spirit for the common good are available to the Body of Christ. In each instance, it is God who works all of them in all men. It just isn't me. It never is. It is always Him.

Since it is never me, I can be certain that the healer is God Himself. If I cannot "do it" myself, likely I cannot mess it up either.

Since I am not "doing it" I can have absolute assurance that you, with a little practice, can learn to "not do it" either.

A Final Word on Tongues

I believe that all believers who ask Jesus for the Baptism in the Holy Spirit receive it. We have His word on it.

> *"So I say to you: Ask and it will be given to you; seek and you will find; knock and the door will be opened to you. For everyone who asks receives; he who seeks finds; and to him who knocks, the door will be opened . . . . If you then, though you are evil, know how to give good gifts to your children, how much more will your Father in heaven give the Holy Spirit to those who ask him!"* (Luke 11:9-13)

> *God gives the Spirit without limit.* (John 3:34)

29

I also believe that each believer receives an invaluable gift of a private prayer language. You may choose to use it or you may leave it dormant. It will not be forced on you.

Your private prayer language enables your spirit to communicate perfectly with the Spirit of God. Although you will not know what you are saying, this gift of perfect communication is a great comfort and blessing to many.

Nancy and I have not discerned a value of use of the private prayer language in praying for healing, miracles or salvation. In none of these instances are we praying for something that exceeds our understanding. I am not saying we understand what needs to be done. I am saying that, in each instance, we know exactly WHO needs to act for anything to happen. A private prayer language does not seem to be necessary to ask Jesus to heal a person from every disease or discomfort, to heal the mind and emotions of a person irrespective of the source of the difficulty or to change the destination of that person from hell to heaven.

Because healing seems to be mysterious to many, a common temptation is to pray in tongues for the healing. If you don't know how to pray, use your private prayer language. However, when you grasp the concepts discussed in this book, you will know exactly what to pray.

A lot of people for whom we have prayed want to pray with their private prayer language while we are praying for healing. We discourage this practice. We discourage the person who is receiving healing from praying at all unless it is a prayer for salvation.

Salvation, healing and delivery from torment in your mind and emotions are all gifts from God. You cannot earn a gift. We explain to people before we pray for them that we will not be working hard praying for them because we cannot earn it. Likewise, they need not pray because they cannot earn it.

God gives his gifts of healing and delivery from torment in our mind and emotions simply because He wants to. Thus, the title to this book, Because He Said So. You are not going to be healed because I can, through your or my prayer, convince God you are a worthy object of His compassion. You are already a worthy object of His compassion, Because He Said So.

We do not pray to change God's mind. His mind is already made up on this subject.

We do not beg God for healing. He already wants to do that, and indeed has already put it in place. If I beg God for healing, I am presuming that my compassion is greater than God's compassion, a simply ludicrous proposition.

Ask Again

We urge all who want to experience miracles, signs and wonders to ask again for Baptism in the Holy Spirit. There are two reasons we recommend this.

The first, and probably most important, reason is that we leak. Our experience is that we need a continual filling and a continual renewing of the Holy Spirit upon us. Don't feel that you have to do anything wrong in order to leak. You leak simply because it is the nature of your bucket.

The second reason we recommend you ask again is that many people in our experience seek Baptism in the Holy Spirit with an emphasis on the gift of tongues. We know that on a denominational basis tongues is often an issue. We also know that many churches teach Baptism in the Holy Spirit with the initial evidence of speaking in tongues. We recognize that, to put it mildly, the subject of tongues is a confusing issue for many Christians.

We urge people to pray for Baptism in the Holy Spirit with an emphasis on asking for each of the gifts enumerated in 1

Corinthians 12. Rather than focusing exclusively or primarily on tongues, we recommend and pray for an equipping by the Holy Spirit for each of the gifts. For many in our classes, this approach is brand new. They simply have not thought it possible to request the fullness of the Holy Spirit when asking for Baptism in the Holy Spirit.

Our experience in our classes is that the spirit of Wisdom and Revelation is released or at least enhanced when approaching Baptism in the Holy Spirit as an invitation to the full banquet table in the kingdom.

CHAPTER THREE
Surprised by God

As we changed our way of thinking to embrace the truth of the concepts addressed in this book, we started seeing a surprisingly high percentage of people healed when we prayed for them. We were pretty careful about who we approached for prayer. Our selection criteria had as much to do with avoiding fearful, embarrassing situations as anything else. Mainly our activities were restricted to either our church or our home.

After a few months we encountered a test of our desire to participate in delivering God's compassion to His people. We had not yet dared to approach a complete stranger in any other arena.

We like to eat breakfast at La Madeleine in Fort Worth. The drive to Fort Worth from Granbury gives us some time to get away from the press of legal work and the daily grind of life in Granbury. We also enjoy the food.

We had been going to La Madeleine often enough to start to recognize some faces but not often enough to have developed even a nodding acquaintance with anyone. One of the men I noticed there nearly every time we went was an elderly man who walked with a cane and clearly was significantly impaired. The hitch in his get-a-long made it obvious he walked with a lot pain.

I found myself sitting where I would have to look directly at this man nearly each time we saw him. Either he would already be there and we would sit close by or he would come after we were located and sit close to us. He seemed to always sit alone and never seemed to be in a good mood. We called him the curmudgeon.

I began to sense that God was directing me to pray for this man. In order to avoid praying for him, I would ask Nancy whether she had heard that we were supposed to pray for him. She was as reluctant as me. Her normal response was, "I don't get those messages, you do." She was fairly certain she had not received any such direction. So, on several occasions we left the restaurant without approaching the curmudgeon, greatly relieved that we had not been inconvenienced or embarrassed by approaching him with an offer of prayer.

On each of those occasions, I would feel "hounded" by God all the way back to Granbury. I was embarrassed that I let my concerns for my reputation and my comfort override what was becoming a clear direction to pray for this man. Finally I told Nancy on the way back to Granbury, "The next time we see that guy at La Madeleine I am going to offer to pray for him. I am tired of fighting God all the way back home."

On our next trip to La Madeleine I hoped all the way there that he would not be there. When we arrived, he was not there, much to my relief. I was very threatened when he walked through the door. We ate very slowly to see if maybe he would finish and leave before we finished our food. The attempted dodge didn't work.

On this occasion, he was not sitting alone but rather was at a table with three other folks we had never seen before. Oh great, I thought. Now we get to be embarrassed before an audience.

After we finished our breakfast, I looked at Nancy and said, "I will go over there and see if we can pray for him." She agreed to come with me.

On my way to his table, the dread was so thick you could have cut it with a knife. I walked up to the table, stuck out my hand and introduced myself.

The curmudgeon introduced himself as Todd and said, "Well, Jeff, remind me when we met. I have forgotten."

I said, "We just met for the first time." Decision time, what do I do?

I took a deep breath and said, "Todd, the Holy Spirit has had his eye on you for several weeks, at least. God has told me to pray for you on many occasions, which I have not done, and then He would hound me all the way back to Granbury. Would it be alright if my wife and I prayed for you this morning?"

Todd said, "Sure. That would be just fine." The others at his table looked stunned at what was happening.

I asked, "You have quite a hitch in your get-along. What's going on there?"

Todd said he had a World War II injury to his back and his knee was "bone-on bone" which combined to make it quite difficult for him to get around.

I explained, "We have seen God do some amazing things with orthopedic problems. Let's see what He will do this morning."

Nancy and I prayed our best prayer. It was quite short, in large part because of our discomfort in praying in this surrounding and under these circumstances. When we finished we hit the door running. I told Nancy, "At least God is going to leave me alone on the trip home."

We did not ask Todd about the results of the prayer. We did not discern any difference in his condition before we split. We just wanted out of there, and quickly.

The next time we saw Todd was a few days later. I asked if there was any improvement in his condition. He reported none. When we saw him move, none was apparent. I told him that we gave "booster shots" if the first prayer didn't work. I hurriedly offered a follow-up prayer and went on my way.

We continued to see Todd a couple times each week. He was never alone again. His attitude and outlook seemed to be sunny and quite different but his pronounced limp and dependence upon his cane continued. He always spoke to us and inquired how we were doing.

For all outward appearances it seemed that nothing had happened when we prayed for Todd. I was glad just to get God off my back in relation to this old man. However, he did seem considerably more social.

After about nine months, Todd approached our table one morning at La Madeleine. He sat with us and said, "You two are such a cute couple. You really go together well."

I said, "Well thanks." I wondered what was coming. Why was he buttering us up?

He continued, "I usually go to bed about 8:30 each night, not because I am tired but by then the pain is too much to bear so I get off my feet. While I am in bed, I think about the people in my life who have been important to me. I often think of you two. You will never know how much what you did meant to me."

With that, he was gone back to his table. Nancy and I looked at each other in tears. Wow. We had thought nothing had happened when we prayed for Todd. Were we ever wrong!

By the time this book was first in print, we had not seen Todd for nearly a year. I was certain he had died. After all, he was 87 when we first prayed for him. We felt the atmosphere in La Madeleine had changed. A subtle change had come over the older crowd who we would describe as regulars. We attributed that change to Todd's passing.

While this book was at the printers, and therefore out of my hands, we were in La Madeleine and in walked Todd. What a shock and a thrill. I was upset because I had named him in the book believing he had died. If I had known he was still alive and might read the book, I would not have both named him and called him a curmudgeon in the same chapter.

I gave him a big hug. Nancy visited quickly with him and explained that I had written this book which discussed him. She promised we would visit more with him after our breakfast.

We noticed that Todd was sitting at a table with many men who he previously refused to sit with. Literally everyone who came by his table has something to say to him. We learned that he had recently had his 90th birthday party. All the men at that table had comments about the party.

When we visited with Todd, I explained that I was embarrassed that we had called him a curmudgeon. His immediate response was, "That's just not true."

I explained that he had appeared to be a curmudgeon and was quite a fearful figure for me.

He said, "My wife and my daughter always told me that I was a scary person."

"You certainly were to me," I said.

We discussed that we had not seen any change in him upon the occasion of our first prayers for him. He said, "Oh, I knew immediately that something had happened."

We learned several important lessons in our dealings with Todd. Todd was the first person we prayed for "as we went." He was in our midst but not in our church environment. The impulse to pray for him was significantly different from what we had experienced in the prayer line at church or in healing sessions at our home. No one had brought him to us for prayer. The experience with Todd taught us to be on the lookout for opportunities to pray for God's compassion on His people in everyday situations and unlikely places.

The Parable of the Minas

We both recognize the circumstances surrounding our relationship with Todd were a test from God to see whether we were really serious about praying for the sick and tormented. I had no question God was instructing me to pray for Todd. Were we willing only to pray when it was convenient for us? Were we willing to pray only when we could feel God's anointing presence with us? Were we willing to pray, armed only with the authority God gives all believers?

We have come to refer to such tests as minas. In Luke 19:12-26, Jesus told the parable of the minas. A man of noble birth dispersed considerable wealth upon each of his ten servants before he went to a distant country to be appointed king and then to return. The measure of the money was a mina, about 1,000 dollars, quite a treasure at the time.

Upon his return, the king demanded an accounting. The first servant reported, *"Sir, your mina has earned ten more."* Notice the servant attributed the work and the increase to the mina, not to himself or his actions. The servant recognized that, at all times, the mina belonged to the king.

The king's response was enigmatic. He said, *"Well done, my good servant! Because you have been trustworthy in a very small matter, take charge of ten cities."* The reward for simply permitting the king's treasure to work in his kingdom was not more treasure but rather a monumental increase in authority in the kingdom. Permitting the king's treasure to do its work and respecting the ownership of the treasure led to greater authority in the kingdom.

Nancy and I recognize many situations as minas. When we are presented with a challenge in the kingdom we treat it as a mina. We are convinced that God is constantly checking up with us to see whose agenda has top priority. We are almost frightened to let our agenda overrule His agenda. When He presents an opportunity to us to do something, we go straight ahead without fear of failure. We don't want to have our authority reduced.

The final servant discussed in the parable of the minas laid away the mina out of fear of the king. His discussion with the king shows clearly he did not understand the essential nature of the king. He thought the king was a hard man. This mistaken evaluation of the king prevented him from acting boldly with the king's treasure. The result was that the mina was taken from him and given to the servant with the ten minas.

No Need to Wait for the Anointing

Our experience with Todd taught us that sensing the anointing for healing that is common in the prayer line with the organ playing in the background is unnecessary when God is delivering His compassion to His people. We knew that we have been given authority to pray for people who are sick or suffering irrespective of whether we first sense the presence of God or His healing power.

We know that all believers have been given this authority. How do we know? Because He Said So. "Anyone who has faith in me will do those things I have been doing. He will do even greater things than these because I am going to the Father." (John 14:12) "As the Father has sent me, I am sending you." (John 20:21)

God's Purposes Won't Be Frustrated

God is not limited by what we ask for. We asked exclusively for relief from physical symptoms for Todd because that is what we saw. God manifested healing of Todd's mind and emotions, a delivery from torment. Did we miss it? Not really. I knew that God was prompting us to pray for Todd. I never bothered to ask what to pray. I simply assumed that what I saw, my agenda was His agenda. We have learned to avoid that mistake.

Paul described God as "him who is able to do immeasurably more than all we ask or imagine, according to his power that is at work within us." (Ephesians 3:20) Our limitations did not limit God's power. We did not ask for what was delivered. We did not imagine that God was working on Todd's heart rather than on his back and knee. Our limitations did not limit God. He delivered His compassion to Todd right where Todd needed it.

Impossible for Nothing to Happen

Our experience with Todd also taught us that it is impossible for nothing to happen when we pray consistent with God's will. Prayers for healing of the physical body, the mind or emotions have the backing of all of heaven. It is not possible that God will not act on the authority He has given to "anyone who has faith in Jesus." Authority without the power of the one granting the authority is no authority at all.

Although we saw no immediate result in Todd, and never saw the result that we asked for, there is no question that Todd's life was changed. He was no longer a curmudgeon. Not only was he changed, the entire atmosphere surrounding him was changed.

When we are met with the initial disappointment of not seeing the result we hoped, we are careful to celebrate that God is working even though His work was not yet evident to us. We do not let that initial disappointment prevent us from praying for others as we go.

CHAPTER FOUR

How Did Jesus Do That?

One product of a renewed mind is a proper view of **how** Jesus did **what** He did **while** He walked the earth. If you believe that Jesus was able to perform miracles, signs and wonders because He is God, you will find it hard to accept Jesus' promise that *"anyone who has faith in me will do what I have been doing."* (John 14:12) You will look for an out. You will search for a definition of "anyone" that does not include you. You will find it very hard to take Jesus at His word.

If, however, you are willing to accept that Jesus operated on earth under self-imposed limitations, the possibilities become limitless. Coupled with these limitless possibilities comes a charge and responsibility to act in the kingdom as you have been authorized to act.

Self Imposed Limitations

Let's be very clear. Jesus is now and has always been God. (John 1:1) However, while Jesus walked the earth as a man, He set aside most of His prerogatives. He imposed these limitations on Himself.

"Like what?" you ask. God is omnipresent, He is everywhere. While walking this earth, Jesus was not omnipresent. He was not physically present in Samaria at the same time He was physically present in Jerusalem.

God is omniscient or all knowing. While He was here, Jesus was not. Someone who is all knowing cannot be surprised. Jesus was not only surprised, He was astonished. (Matthew 8:10) Someone who is omniscient already knows all things and cannot learn new things. However, Jesus learned about the condition of the invalid beside the pool of Bethesda. (John 5:6)

"Wait," you say. We are not in the same situation as Jesus. Surely He was able to heal everyone who came to Him because He was God. Since we are not God, we cannot expect to be able to heal anyone. That is solely God's province. The proper response to this argument is "Yes" and "No."

> The "Yes": It has always been and always will be the province of God to provide the power to heal and deliver from torment.
>
> The "No": Jesus, the man, had no power to heal. He could not raise the dead. He could not deliver from torment. He could not cast out demons. With His self-imposed limitations He stood before the Father as we do.

Nonetheless, Jesus was God. He was the exact representation of the Father. (Hebrews 1:3) All the fullness of God Himself lived in Jesus. (1 Colossians 2:9) Yet, Jesus was made like us in every way. (Hebrews 2:17)

Since Jesus is God, how can I say that Jesus had no power to heal, could not raise the dead, deliver from torment or cast out demons under his own power? I say that Because He Said So.

After healing the invalid by the pool of Bethesda, (John, Chapter 5) Jesus was questioned about healing on the Sabbath. (Don't religious leaders amaze you? Forget the fact that the invalid was healed. Let's be religious and question the day of the week rather than be astounded at the power of God.) Jesus gave them this answer:

> *"I tell you the truth, the Son can do nothing by Himself; he can do only what he sees his Father doing, because whatever the Father does the Son also does."* (John 5:19)

This statement deals directly with power and authority, not choice or volition. Jesus didn't say He chose not to do anything unless He saw the Father doing it. He said He *could not* do anything by Himself. If I take Jesus at His word, Jesus had no power to do anything by Himself. While He walked the earth, Jesus was completely dependent upon the power of the Holy Spirit.

Jesus Modeled Behavior

Jesus' actions were not principally designed to illustrate the power of God. God's power was recorded and well recognized throughout the Old Testament. Jesus did not need to do one thing to illustrate that God was able to do all He needed to do to accomplish His purposes.

Jesus' actions modeled the power made available to a man standing in right relation to God. If the same right relation to God is available to us, we have a perfect model of what we can expect to accomplish in the kingdom.

How Did Jesus Pray?

How do you suppose Jesus prayed? What guidance and direction did He seek from the Father? Because He was not omnipresent, Jesus had to rely on the Father to position Him where God was going to act and direct Him what to do. I believe that a lot of Jesus' prayer time was dedicated to discovering where God was directing Him to go next and who the focus of God's attention in that place would be.

We can pray for the exact same guidance and direction. Although God is omnipresent, He is not acting through us throughout the world. Rather, His action through us necessarily occurs where we are. Just like Jesus, we need to understand where we need to be and who the objects of God's compassion are before we will be able to participate as co-laborers with God in any situation.

Baptism by John

Every miracle, sign and wonder performed by Jesus followed His baptism by John. When He came out of the water, scripture records the Spirit of God descended upon him like a dove **and remained.** (John 1:33) Peter explained the source of Jesus' power this way:

> *You know what has happened throughout Judea, beginning in Galilee after the baptism that John preached—how God anointed Jesus of Nazareth with the Holy Spirit and power, and how he went around doing good and healing all who were under the power of the devil, because God was with him.* (Acts 10:37-38)

Jesus relied upon the Holy Spirit for all the power He needed to accomplish what the Father desired. Peter emphasizes that *God anointed Jesus with the Holy Spirit and with power.* We have access to the very same power. Peter finishes with the reminder that Jesus did all He did *because God was with him.* If the Holy Spirit was not present to act, Jesus got nothing done. The Holy Spirit was the source of the power to do those things the Father was doing. When Jesus testified that He could only do what He saw the Father doing He was admitting that unless the Father had sent the Holy Spirit to perform miracles, signs and wonders, there would be no miracles, signs and wonders. It is God who performed the miracles, signs and wonders through the power of the Holy Spirit, not Jesus the man.

On the day of Pentecost, Peter said: *"Jesus of Nazareth was a man accredited by God to you by miracles, wonders and signs, which God did among you through him, as you yourselves know."* (Acts 2:22) Jesus did not perform the miracles, wonders and signs. Rather, God performed the miracles, wonders and signs. He performed those miracles, signs and wonders by acting *through* Jesus. God was the actor, not Jesus. Jesus was the perfect vessel. Jesus was a perfect host for the *presence* of God. The Spirit *remained* on Him.

Luke, the author of both the Gospel of Luke and the Book of the Acts of the Apostles, was a physician. With his medical background, Luke is likely a trustworthy reporter of the nature of the healings he described. Luke recounts the healing of an invalid lowered through a roof on his bed to be placed in front of Jesus.

> *One day as he was teaching, Pharisees and teachers of the law, who had come from every village of Galilee and from Judea and Jerusalem, were sitting there. And the power of the Lord was present for him to heal the sick.* (Luke 5:17)

Luke knew full well that by Himself Jesus could do nothing. How did he know? Jesus told him! Luke also knew that when Jesus saw what the Father was doing, all things were possible. Thus, Luke records that *the power of the Lord was present for him to heal the sick.* Absent this power, nothing would have happened. How do I know that? Because He Said So.

Not only was Jesus able to do only what He saw the Father doing, He was very careful about his tongue. Jesus only said what He heard the Father saying. Jesus said, "*I do nothing on my own but speak just what the Father has taught me.*" (John 5:28) Jesus did not claim to speak of His own authority. He claimed that the Father commanded Him not only what to say but also how to say it. (John 12:49)

Jesus was not guarding His tongue to avoid sinning by His words. He guarded His tongue because He recognized that His words had extraordinary power. Jesus said, "*The words I have spoken to you are spirit and they are life.*" (John 6:63) Peter confessed that Jesus had "*the words of eternal life.*" (John 6:67). If Jesus spoke it, it came to pass. It came to pass because Jesus only said what He heard the Father saying in the manner the Father told Him to say it. Isn't that the very definition of prophecy? Prophecy is saying the words of God in the manner God has instructed.

The Power of Prophecy

God's word, once spoken, has power to accomplish God's purposes. God spoke the world into existence. God's word has incredible power and does not return to Him void.

> "*My word that goes out from my mouth . . . will not return to me empty, but will accomplish what I desire and achieve the purpose for which I sent it.* (Isaiah 55:11)

If God didn't say it, it isn't prophecy. It may be an accurate prediction of the future but it is not prophecy unless God says it.

A prophet is only a spokesman, not an interpreter. Spokesmen, by definition, speak for others, not themselves. Spokesmen give utterance to words, ideas and concepts that have no reality unless authorized by the person sending the spokesman. Spokesmen have no power to bring their words to pass unless the one for whom they speak has that power.

In this context, let's look at a powerful verse from The Revelation of Jesus Christ.

> *"For the testimony of Jesus is the spirit of prophecy."*
> (Revelation 19:10)

The phrase *"the testimony of Jesus is the spirit of prophecy"* is one of those powerful truths from the Bible that I recognized as extremely important when I first heard it but was unable to comprehend. I knew something enormous was contained in that phrase but couldn't comprehend what it was. Merely uttering that phrase in our study group ushered in a nearly tangible awareness of the presence of God. The mystery continues to unfold as we continue to ask God for miracles, signs and wonders.

Prophecy, the word of God, changes the reality of the circumstances in which it is uttered. The word of God has the power and authority of heaven behind it. Prophecy brings the presence of God and all His power with it. It is impossible to separate the *presence* of God from the *power* of God. When Jesus knew the Spirit of the Lord was *present*, He knew the *power* of the Lord was available for Him to heal the sick.

What is the *testimony of Jesus*? I do not claim to have anything near a complete understanding of the reach of the *testimony of Jesus*. I am certain, however, that, at a minimum, the testimony of Jesus includes what Jesus said (His words), what Jesus did in biblical times and what Jesus is doing today.

We have definitely perceived a pattern. When we recite the testimony of what Jesus has been doing in our midst, more miraculous healings occur while we are praying for others. It seems the closer the current prayer is to the testimony recited, the more likely a miracle is on the way.

I have no explanation why there is power in giving the testimony of Jesus. I am simply reporting that the testimony of Jesus ushers in an *awareness* of the *presence* of God. The spirit of prophecy is released by recitation of the testimony of Jesus. Since Jesus is the same, yesterday, today and forever (Hebrews 13:8), if Jesus did it in biblical times, last week or an hour ago, we can be certain that what the Father was doing in the past is consistent with His will and nature and He will continue doing it today.

The Power of the Testimony

Our experience with the Testimony of Jesus started with Lynda. Nancy and I dropped by to see Lynda after a movie one day in Granbury. Nancy's hands and my back had been healed less than one month at this time. We visited with her about her life, family and business, all of which were in turmoil. God gave us many words of knowledge about her situation and some wisdom which we shared with her. We also shared the Testimony of Jesus about Nancy's hands and my back.

Lynda had a damaged rotator cuff in her left shoulder. This was a particular problem for her because she is a massage therapist. She believed that God did heal some people. She was not at all sure that God would heal her because of her personal history.

Lynda's shoulder was so bad that she had to support her left elbow with her right hand and hold her arm close to her body while on a trip to Mexico. When she returned, Nancy and I had occasion to pray for her shoulder. She got some relief but not total relief. We offered to pray again. She was not willing for a repeat prayer at that time. She said, "I know God can do this. We have already prayed. I will just wait for Him."

A few days later, Nancy and I again were with Lynda. We told her once again that Nancy's hands were healed after two short prayers. We reminded her that when Jesus prayed for a man who was blind and then inquired how the man could see he reported he saw men as trees walking. Jesus' response was to pray again. (Mark 8:24) We were going to pray again. If Jesus could pray twice, so could we. While we were riding in the car, we reached over the front seat to get our hands on Lynda once again.

We found our way to Chili's for lunch with Lynda. While we were at lunch Lynda was moving her shoulder around, explaining she was just waiting for God to answer the prayers. Quickly she realized she had full movement in her shoulder and no pain. Her verbal response let everyone in Chili's know that God was awesome.

Nearly one year later we had occasion to record some testimonies of God's healing power. Lynda was there to give her testimony. She told the audience about her left shoulder problem and demonstrated the freedom of movement she still had with no pain. Then she explained that she had recently fallen in Costco while shopping and injured her right shoulder. She demonstrated the limitation in movement in that shoulder and said, "Maybe tonight when we pray God will fix this one."

She did not mention that she had the results of a recent MRI in her car with her that night showing two complete tears of muscles in her right rotator cuff. She was in the middle of submitting a claim to Costco for her injuries.

After the healing service, Lynda was praying for others. During that time, one of the women there began to pray for Lynda's right shoulder. When she checked for improvement Lynda found she could now raise her right shoulder completely and easily with full range of motion and no pain. God is so awesome.

Good News Travels

Shortly after our experience with Lynda, we visited Ron and Doris Thomson who had moved back to El Paso. We had taken along a video of the healing service we conducted in Granbury. At the end of the video were several testimonies, including a broken back, emotional healing concerning a relationship, healing of a severely sprained ankle requiring crutches, healing of a woman injured throughout her body in a car accident and Lynda's first shoulder experience. We added the report of what had happened that night to the testimony of her shoulder.

When Doris saw Lynda and we discussed the power of the testimony she asked, "Could we go pray for Judy, a member of my Thursday morning Bible study?"

We were overjoyed at the opportunity. Ron, Doris, Nancy and I drove to Judy's house and played the video for her and her husband. Once we saw the testimony of the rotator cuff healing we explained what little we understood about the power of the testimony of Jesus.

We asked Judy to show us how much she could move her arm and shoulder. She was virtually frozen in place. She had complete tears in one or more muscles and was scheduled for surgery.

The group of us prayed for her and asked her to "check it out." She had marginally more movement but was still very impaired. I explained about the blind man Jesus prayed for who saw men as trees walking (Mark 8:24) and that we were going to pray again. If Jesus could pray twice, so could we.

After the second short prayer, Judy smoothly and easily raised her arm straight above her head with no pain. We all watched in awe of the power of God and the reliability of His willingness to heal His people.

Personal Testimony

I have had three surgeries on my left shoulder from 1967 to 1996. God healed my shoulder in the summer of 2010. The rest of that story is included in Chapter 13. I gave my testimony of this healing in our church. The good news was well received.

The Next Step

The following Sunday a woman was called forward for a testimony. We had never met her or spoken with her.

She reported, "Last week I heard the testimony of Jeff Thompson. I have the same problem. When I went home after the service, I got my husband to watch it again on the internet since he had not been in church with me. After watching the testimony again, I discovered that God had healed my shoulder too."

The good news was well received.

Neither Nancy nor I remember her reporting that anyone prayed for her shoulder to be healed. Merely the testimony of Jesus had made the difference.

Another Shoulder

After the service that second Sunday, Debbie, the wife of one of our elders, approached Nancy and me and requested that we pray for her shoulder also since she was scheduled in a short time for surgery on her rotator cuff. We prayed our best prayer and she got partial relief.

I said, "If you would come to our house in Granbury and let our group pray for you there may be a better result."

She was scheduled to travel to San Antonio to visit family that evening so she missed our Sunday night get together. The following week Debbie and her husband visited our group. The prayer for her shoulder was short but it was preceded by a recounting of what God had done for me and for the lady the following week. When the group prayed, God healed her shoulder completely. We asked her to check it out. She could lift her arm straight overhead with not pain. Further, the pain she had been experiencing in her neck was gone.

The following day, the elder's wife called her surgeon's office to cancel the surgery. The nurse suggested a rescheduling of the surgery. She declined, saying Jesus had healed her and she would need no surgery.

The nurse then inquired about her neck which was to be her next surgery. She reported that her neck had also been healed. She needed no surgery.

The following Sunday she gave her testimony about God healing her shoulder and neck. The good news was well received.

The Hits Just Keep On Coming

Soon thereafter I received a call from a friend in Ruidoso who had a friend, Jan, in the DFW Metroplex area with significant problems that were "destroying her life." She asked if her friend could attend our Sunday night meeting.

Jan called for directions for her 75 mile journey on Sunday night. When she arrived she reported that her husband had a bi-polar episode about a year before, during which he had seriously injured her left side. Her major problems were pain in the left shoulder which prevented any substantial movement and pain in the left hip.

We explained the results we had seen with shoulder injuries. We were beginning to be pretty confident God was healing shoulders. The group prayed for her and then asked her to "check it out." She was able to raise her left hand straight over her head with no pain and was quite overcome with that result. We then asked about her hip. She literally ran around the living room to demonstrate that she had no hip pain.

Healing Via Cell Phone

One week later we were with Debbie and her husband on a week night. Jan called, in tears. She reported that she had been perfectly healed but had fallen on the ice outside her apartment. She had spent the last three days crying in her chair because she had injured her shoulder again and was unable to function without pain. She wondered, "Can you pray again?"

Debbie had not been with us when we prayed for Jan. I put Jan on the speaker phone on my cell phone and asked Debbie to give Jan the testimony of what Jesus had done for her and then we would pray for her over the phone. Debbie began her testimony and then slipped into praying for Jan. Her husband, Nancy and I joined in with that prayer.

After the short cell phone prayer, we had Jan "check it out." She reported she could raise her arm again but was experiencing a burning sensation when she did so.

We reminded her that when Jesus prayed for the blind man who saw men as trees walking, Jesus prayed again. So, we prayed again. This time when Jan checked it out she had no pain and could raise her arm fully and completely. Apparently the cell phone and 75 miles distance was no obstacle for the testimony of Jesus.

God Is Amazing

Billy is a lawyer from Texarkana who I had met on a couple of occasions. We found ourselves working on the same side of a case in Dallas along with a long-time friend of mine from El Paso. While we all were in a conference room in Dallas trying to negotiate a settlement to the lawsuit, I received a call from the publisher of this book about the cover design. Since we were simply waiting for the other side to respond to our offer, I took the call.

Billy listened to my side of the call and then said, "It's obvious you are talking about a book. What's that all about?"

I debated explaining the subject of the book. I didn't know Billy well. The El Paso lawyer I did know well and did not expect he would be supportive. We had two clients with us who had no idea really who I was and what my priorities were. I looked at Nancy and decided to come clean.

I explained that the book was about miracles, signs and wonders and no one left the room. I went on to recount the full story of my shoulder and the other related miracles we had seen just in that arena. Billy's eyes were nailed to mine. He said often, "I'd really like to read that book."

We settled the case. It was time to go home. We left the conference room. I shook Billy's hand, Nancy patted him on the arm and we said our good-bys.

We went to the parking lot across the street and found we were parked close to Billy's car. He was giving a ride to the El Paso lawyer so he was also there. I knew the El Paso lawyer was having heart problems and asked him to keep in touch about that. He said, "I just need to come to Saint Peter's house on Sunday night." This was just the kind of mocking I had expected from him.

Billy said, "I just think I want him to touch me." Again, I thought he was mocking us.

We got in our car and returned to Granbury. The next morning I got out of the shower to answer a call from Billy. He said, "Jeff, this will be the strangest call you have ever had."

I said, "Billy, I have practiced law for 37 years, you will have to go some for the strangest call."

He said, "Let me just first say that you and your wife are on fire."

"We are certainly very excited and having the time of our lives," I said.

"You know, when we left each other, you shook my hand and Nancy touched my arm. I got in the car and drove to Texarkana from Dallas. I have a serious back problem that I don't tell people about. I just suffer through because I have already done all that can be done. Well, when I arrived in Texarkana and got out of the car, my back was healed."

I explained that I was not the least surprised. I explained about the testimony of Jesus and the power we had witnessed just from the testimony alone.

He was quite surprised that I was not surprised. Although I was not surprised I was completely in awe of how much God loves us and how willing He is to heal His people. We didn't even know Billy had a problem. No one had prayed for him. Yet, God knew exactly what he needed and delivered His compassion without our even asking. Talk about being powerful to do exceedingly, abundantly more than we can ask or imagine. He is outrageously good, loving and generous with His compassion.

The Power of Our Testimony

Before leaving the subject of testimony, let's examine another statement from the Book of Revelation.

> "They overcame him by the blood of the Lamb
> and by the word of their testimony; they did not
> love their lives so much as to shrink from death."
> (Revelation 12:10-11)

The accuser of the brethren was overcome by blood of the Lamb and the word of their testimonies.

The sacrificed blood of the Lamb paid the price required by the Law, *in full.* The word of the testimonies of our brothers relates to what Jesus has done and is doing in the lives of believers. The collective "word of their testimonies" is the testimony of Jesus, the spirit of prophecy. The collective word of our testimonies is a powerful force because it has the power and authority of heaven behind it.

The word of our testimony furnishes a completion of the promises from God.

> *For the Son of God, Jesus Christ . . . was not "Yes"*
> *and "No," but in him it has always been "Yes."*
> *For no matter how many promises God has made,*
> *they are "Yes" in Christ. And so through him*
> *the "Amen" is spoken by us to the glory of God.*
> (2 Corinthians 1:19-20)

Jesus is the divine Yes to every promise of God. How could He be anything other than the divine Yes? If God had promised it, Jesus must furnish the divine Yes. Otherwise, it cannot be a promise. However, Paul makes it clear that God awaits a response from us. Granted, He is the one who enables us to utter the Amen but God waits for us to say Amen. Our response should match Mary's. *"I am the Lord's servant. May it be to me as you have said."* (Luke 1:38)

CHAPTER FIVE

Clarity of Thought

God anointed Jesus of Nazareth with the Holy Spirit and with power and he went around doing good, healing all who were under the power of the devil because God was with Him. (Acts 10:38)

Today, Jesus has no limitation on His power and authority. While it is true that Jesus set aside His prerogatives as God while He walked the earth, following His resurrection there is a new sheriff in town. The only limitations Jesus ever had were those He imposed.

When Jesus was tempted in the wilderness following His baptism by John, the liar made an interesting statement.

> *"I will give you all their authority and splendor, for it has been given to me, and I can give it to anyone I want to. So if you worship me, it will all be yours."* (Luke 4:6-7)

Jesus did not debate the issue with him. He did not correct him. It is true that the authority of the kingdoms of the world had been given to the liar at some point. Adam and Eve surrendered authority and dominion over the earth to the liar in the Garden. The fall made Adam and Eve (and us) slaves to sin. When one becomes a slave, the slave's prior possessions now belong to the slave owner.

During His walk on earth, Jesus made it clear that He could do nothing by Himself. He could only do what He saw the Father doing. (John 5:19) He only said what He heard the Father say. (John 5:28; John 12:49). After His death and resurrection Jesus came to His eleven disciples and said, "All authority in heaven and on earth has been given to me." (John 28:18) A careful study of the Greek word translated "all" in this passage reveals that it means "all." Since Jesus was given all authority, there was no authority left for the liar.

He then gave the Great Commission, "Therefore go and make disciples of all nations, baptizing them in the name of the Father and of the Son and of the Holy Spirit, and teaching them to obey everything I have commanded you. And surely I am with you always, to the very end of the age." (Matthew 28:19-20) Jesus commissioned the Apostles to teach all nations to obey everything Jesus had commanded them. This command extended the commissioning to us.

We have seen in the previous chapter that Jesus was subject to self-imposed limitations on His power. He relied upon the power of the Holy Spirit to accomplish those things the Father was doing. This reliance on the power of the Holy Spirit is one of the essential elements of "how" Jesus was sent by the Father.

On the evening of the day of His resurrection, Jesus came and stood among the disciples who were hiding behind locked doors in fear that they might be next. Recognizing their fearful condition, Jesus said, *"Peace be with you! As the Father has sent me,*

*I am sending you." And with that he breathed on them and said,
"Receive the Holy Spirit."* (John 20:21-22)

With all authority in heaven and on earth, Jesus commissioned
his Apostles and, through them, us. Jesus sends us just as the
Father sent Jesus. We are sent, like Jesus, wholly dependent upon
the power of the Holy Spirit to accomplish God's purposes on
the earth.

What are we supposed to do with this power? Just like Jesus,
we can only do what the Father is doing and then only through
the power of the Holy Spirit. Jesus promised that anyone with
faith in Him would do the things He had been doing, and greater
things than those.

Jesus was made manifest to destroy the works of the devil.
(1 John 3:8) Our job, in doing those things Jesus had been doing,
is to keep up the fight against the works of the devil. Jesus won
the war. He declared from the cross, "It is finished." (John 19:30)
We know that the battle is over because of the mental picture
painted for us by Paul:

> *And having disarmed the powers and authorities,
> he made a public spectacle of them, triumphing over
> them by the cross.* (Colossians 2:15)

I can see Jesus riding in the victory parade with all the powers
and authorities imprisoned in cages riding behind Him. How
great and powerful He is and how small and insignificant they
are!

Important Concepts in Healing

It is interesting to compare the experience of those who believe
the ideas set out below and those who do not. Those who believe
this theology see God perform miracles, signs and wonders on a

regular, recurring basis. Those who do not believe this theology, by and large, have a different experience.

Theological concepts that open the door to seeing God perform His miracles, signs and wonder include:

o   Jesus is the healer;
o   Healing rests on Christ's Atonement; and
o   Disease and torment are never God's will.

It is not necessary to agree with these theological statements in order to be saved. Your salvation is not the least threatened if you disagree with one or all of those statements.

All Sickness Is From the Devil

God is good—all the time. And, all the time—God is good! Any suggestion that God is the author of sickness or torment flies in the face of this truth.

John Alexander Dowie, a minister with massive experience in healing in the 1800s taught that "Disease, like sin, is God's enemy, and the devil's work and can never be God's will." (Dowie, *Talks With Ministers on Divine Healing*, Congregational Club meeting held in the parlors of the Y.M.C.A. in San Francisco as reported by G.H. Hawkes). It just makes sense that God the Father will not send sickness upon His people when, at the same time, He sent Jesus to destroy the works of the devil. Since Jesus healed **all** who sought healing from Him, we can be certain that the Father's will did not include putting sickness on His people.

As Peter explained, *"God anointed Jesus of Nazareth with the Holy Spirit and with power and he went around doing good, healing all who were under the power of the devil because God was with Him."* (Acts 10:38) This explanation shows clearly that Jesus healed **all** and the source of the difficulty for those being healed was the devil.

There is clarity of purpose that emerges when we recognize that all sickness, disease and torment are the work of the devil. Understanding the source helps us pray with confidence that we are not asking God to countermand any prior order He may have given. We are at complete liberty to oppose sickness and torment without fear that God is author of either of them.

Since *"Jesus Christ is the same yesterday and today and forever"* (Hebrews 13:8), and He went around healing all who were under the power of the devil, He is still in that business. (See John G. Lake, *God's Way of Healing*.)

No Exclusivity

All believers should expect to experience miraculous answers to prayer, not just a select few. We have Jesus' word on it:

> *I tell you the truth, anyone who has faith in me will do what I have been doing. He will do even greater things than these, because I am going to the Father. And I will do whatever you ask in my name, so that the Son may bring glory to the Father. You may ask me for anything in my name, and I will do it.* (John 14:12-14)

This promise makes it abundantly clear that *anyone* who has faith in Jesus is equally qualified to do what Jesus did. It likewise makes clear that *we ask* and *Jesus does*. The power is not in the asking, it is in the doing.

Before my mind was renewed, I had a flawed view of spiritual gifts. Somehow I believed that spiritual gifts gave an ability to the person receiving the gift which enabled that person to perform tasks. If, for example, a person had received a gift of healing I expected that there was a measure of power residing in that person individually to bring forth healing. That view is a significant impediment to participation in supernatural ministry.

This flawed view of spiritual gifts fosters a feeling of exclusivity. If I believe that only certain, select individuals have received the gifts of healing, I will not feel led to pray for the sick and tormented. Rather, I will direct that sick or tormented person to someone who has "the gift." If I can escape participation by directing the sick or tormented to others, I have no responsibility in the kingdom to deliver God's compassion to his people.

Healing and Delivery from Torment Are In the Atonement

Divine healing and delivery from torment are in the atonement. The atonement includes a payment for our healing and a delivery from torment. (Isaiah 53:4-5; Matthew 8:17) An atonement that delivers us from the power of the devil necessarily deals with *all* the works of the devil. The atonement is not limited to a change of destination from hell to heaven. It also includes delivery from the power of sickness, disease and torment.

Since the time of Martin Luther, we have been taught that forgiveness of sin is available to all who believe, that saving grace comes through faith, not works. We have not been taught nearly so clearly about physical or emotional healing. Yet, both rest upon the same sacrificial act by Jesus.

We believe that we are "saved" by grace by belief in Jesus. This salvation is a gift given through His sacrificial blood. We don't doubt that "God our Savior . . . wants all men to be saved and to come to a knowledge of the truth." (1 Timothy 2:3-4) Upon a declaration of faith, we fully expect to see a changed life, never doubting that the "sinner's prayer" will deliver saving grace.

Supernatural healing and delivery from torment are gifts from God just like a change of destination from hell to heaven. We do not question this change of destination. We should likewise not question that physical and emotional healing are already ours for the asking. Why should we be slow to accept that the crushing of His body was a payment for our healing? Why do we question that Jesus carried our diseases? (Matthew 8:17; Isaiah 53:4-5) The renewing of your mind permits you to legitimately expect to see God manifest the healing Jesus bought and paid for when you pray for physical or emotional healing.

Healing Cannot be Earned

Since supernatural healing and delivery from torment is a gift, it cannot be earned. Great freedom comes from the proper recognition of this healing and delivery as a gift. The person who is praying does not need to work to earn the gift. The person for whom prayer is offered does not work to receive the gift. If either person is working (by exhibiting the proper attitude, having a positive confession, aligning his mind with the word of God, etc.), they labor in vain. Gifts are given, not earned.

We have noticed that, more often than not, when the person who is asking for prayer then participates in the prayer, often by praying in tongues, the requested healing is not manifested to our senses. We generally are careful to instruct the person for whom we are praying that Nancy and I are going to do nothing. Jesus is the healer, and only Jesus is involved. We are not going to work at anything because we cannot earn the healing we are requesting. Likewise, since healing is a gift, the person for whom we are praying cannot earn the requested healing. We want the person to understand that nothing other than reception is necessary. Any attempt to do more than simply receive the manifestation of the power of God smacks of earning God's favor, something we are incapable of doing.

Many people want to manifest or display their belief by having a "positive confession" while we are praying for them. We likewise view such statements of a positive confession as a form of working for God's healing. We discourage that type of activity during the prayer.

It sometimes seems to help to remind the person for whom we are praying that we are not trying to persuade God to do something He is not already prepared to do. We are not involved in any manner in trying to change God's mind. Consequently, we need not remind God how worthy a subject this person is, how much faith this person has displayed, how many good works this person has performed, how much the congregation does or should love this person or how much the person believes that God will heal him.

Many times people for whom we are about to pray will say, "I believe in healing" or "I believe that God can heal." When the person makes a statement like either of those without prompting, it is our experience that we do not see a present manifestation of the healing we request. Why is that? I am not sure of the answer. It seems that an unsolicited statement of this variety is an expression of an intellectual belief or attempt to believe that God is *capable* of healing coupled with a *measure of doubt* that God will exercise his capability on this person.

There is a difference in a belief in an abstract proposition and knowledge of the truth of the proposition. Likewise, there is a difference in a belief in God and "*a knowledge of the truth.*" (1 Timothy 2:3-4) Jesus said, "*I am the way and the truth and the life.*" (John 14:6) Knowledge of the truth far surpasses a belief in the truth. Knowing God is quite different from believing in God. When I say, "I believe in God," part of me is saying, "I want to believe in God, I want to have faith in God, but I have insufficient experience with Him to say that I know Him; I want and need desperately for God to be real but I am uncertain of Him in my daily walk."

Seeing miracles took Nancy and me out of the realm of I want to believe in this God of the Bible and delivered us into the realm of knowing God is real and is vitally interested in our daily existence. We now know Him well enough to know that He is in the healing business and business is good. We know that the healing store is never closed.

God Is In the Healing Business

When we pray for healing, we are not praying to change God's mind. He has already made up His mind. God is now, and always has been, in the healing business. It is His nature. It is one of His attributes. He is *Jehovah Rapha'*. He is *"the LORD, who heals you."* (Exodus 15:26) We aren't asking God to do something extraordinary in the sense of out of His normal pattern of behavior. Everything He does involves extraordinary power from our perspective. In fact, everything He does is impossible for us to do on our own. That fact that it is impossible does not mean the result we ask for is either improbable or unlikely.

David recognized God as both redeemer and healer.

> *Praise the LORD, O my soul, and forget not all his benefits—who forgives all your sins and heals all your diseases, who redeems your life from the pit and crowns you with love and compassion, who satisfies your desires with good things so that your youth is renewed like the eagle's.* (Psalms 103:2-5)

God does not change. If He was redeeming His people through forgiveness of sins and healing diseases in David's time, He is still forgiving sins and healing diseases now.

Sacrificial System

In the sacrificial system of the Old Testament, forgiveness of sins was obtained by a confession of sins and the offering of the prescribed sacrifice in payment of the penalty for the sin. Once the confession was made and the payment was made, the sins were forgiven.

In the New Testament reality, the order has been reversed. Jesus was the perfect sacrificial lamb who was killed on the cross to pay the price for the forgiveness of all sin. This payment was made once for all. (Romans 6:10; Hebrews 7:27; Hebrews 9:25-28) He will not repeat this action. (Hebrews 9:25) Jesus *cannot* die again since death has lost its mastery over Him. (Romans 6:9)

All sin committed by anyone alive today comes well after the payment. The penalty was already paid, in full, long before the idea of sin was born in any person living today.

Isaiah prophesied that God would place the sin of all mankind on his suffering servant, Jesus, who would settle the issue. "*The LORD has laid on him the iniquity of us all.*" (Isaiah 53:6)

Isaiah knew that we would get it wrong. He prophesied that God's people would consider Jesus as having been stricken by God Himself, not by us. "*Yet, we considered Him stricken by God, smitten by Him and afflicted.*" (Isaiah 53:4) But, Isaiah makes it clear that Jesus was pierced for our transgressions—not His. He was crushed for our iniquities. (Isaiah 53:5) There was no fault on His side of the equation. It was our iniquities which brought these consequences upon Jesus. It is clear that the price paid by Jesus was an advance deposit for the forgiveness of our sins today. Before the sins of today were ever conceived, the door to forgiveness was flung wide open and the entire penalty was paid.

Payment for Healing and Delivery from Torment

Isaiah is just as clear that *surely* Jesus took up our infirmities and carried our diseases. (Isaiah 53:4) (Matthew 8:17) Just as He made a payment in full for the forgiveness of sin, He also made a payment in full for healing and delivery from torment. "*The punishment that brought us peace was upon Him.*" (Isaiah 53:5) The physical beating Jesus endured before being nailed to the cross secured *peace* for us today.

Just as Jesus will not come again for another crucifixion for the forgiveness of sin, He will not endure punishment again for our *peace*. The price for our delivery from torment has already been paid in full.

Jesus' beating also paid for our physical healing. "*By His wounds (stripes) we are healed.*" (Isaiah 53:5) The word translated *healed* in this passage is *rapha'*, which refers to a physical healing. On His way to the cross, Jesus paid the price in full for my physical healing today.

The payments Jesus made for (1) forgiveness of sins, (2) delivery from torment, and (3) physical healing were ENOUGH. Jesus thought of everything and paid for it all.

There is no need to change God's mind about any of those three issues. Since the payment was made in full and encompassed everything, even those things in the future, Jesus settled for all time the issues of sin, torment and healing. "*Jesus Christ is the same yesterday and today and forever.* (Hebrews 13:8) He was fully committed against sin, torment and disease then. He is likewise fully committed today. He will be fully committed forever.

God had a special anointing for Jesus.

> *"The Spirit of the Lord is on me, because he has anointed me to preach good news to the poor. He has sent me to proclaim freedom for the prisoners and recovery of sight for the blind, to release the oppressed, to proclaim the year of the Lord's favor."* (Luke 4:18-19)

He was sent to proclaim freedom, recovery of health (sight for the blind), and release from oppression.

Peter explained it this way:

> *"God anointed Jesus of Nazareth with the Holy Ghost and with power: who went about doing good, and healing all that were oppressed of the devil; for God was with him."* (Acts 10:38 KJV))

Jesus healed *all* who were oppressed by the devil. He *released* the oppressed by *healing* them of their diseases and giving them the peace that passes understanding. The word translated *healing* in this passage is the now familiar *rapha'*. Jesus was the healer then, is the healer now, and will be the healer forever. For God to change His mind on healing, Jesus has to change. God has given his Word that Jesus is not about to change.

No Experts Required

God has not limited His activities in physical or emotional healing to a select few who have received a special anointing. I am *not* saying there is not an anointing for healing. I *am* saying that every believer has the power and authority to pray for divine healing, for himself and others. We have seen in our classes that miracles start on the first class session and result from the prayers of class members with no prior experience with miracles, signs and wonders.

Although Nancy and I have experienced a significant boost in the number of miracles, signs and wonders we have seen, we claim no special ability. Quite the opposite! We know beyond doubt that we are mere pawns on the chessboard of healing and delivery from torment. Just as in chess, all pieces have only one function, to serve the King.

Nancy has become bolder in praying out loud. She felt for many years that she just didn't have the flowery speech and "gift of gab" in her communication with God that she thought she heard in the audible prayers of others. Consequently, although she prayed fervently, she seldom prayed out loud and was almost never the leader in audible prayer.

About three weeks into our pursuit of miracles, signs and wonders, we visited a Thursday night ministry in Ruidoso where I have been permitted to deliver God's message on many occasions. Nancy had been praying for a renewal of God's compassion in her. She just wasn't as moved by the suffering of others as she felt she should be. While at the Thursday night meeting, she was asked to share about the healing of her hands. When she was done sharing, I launched into one of my favorite messages.

In the middle of the message, one of the men in attendance got a phone call—don't you just love cell phones? He had recently had surgery for brain cancer and feared the remission his doctors were reporting was a false report. I had spoken with him before the meal, introducing myself because I was certain from his appearance that we had never met. When he told me his name, I realized this man was someone we had known for a few years. His appearance was so different I had not recognized him.

He apologized for needing to leave and started for the door. I had promised him that we would pray for him before the night was over so I stopped my message and we started praying for him. Many joined in the laying on of hands while we prayed for salvation assurance, physical healing and delivery from torment.

When we concluded our prayers, he turned to Nancy and said, "I want *her* to pray for me. My hands and my feet hurt me so much." Nancy was moved to tears as she asked God to heal his hands and feet and to deliver the shalom of heaven upon this man. He then left and I returned to my message.

In bed in the middle of the night, Nancy lay awake worrying whether she had let this man down due to the "inadequacy" of her prayer. Had she asked confidently enough? Had she demonstrated enough faith? Were the words sufficient? Had the compassion she felt which moved her to tears been delivered? Would this man die because she did something "wrong."

We all recognize it doesn't take an expert to pray with someone for salvation. We don't seek someone with a "special anointing" to lead another in the sinner's prayer for redemption. Yet we tend to believe that it takes an expert, someone uniquely gifted, to pray for healing and delivery from torment.

That Thursday night God told Nancy unmistakably that it doesn't take an expert to pray for healing and delivery from torment. God told Nancy that it didn't matter how she prayed. It didn't matter what words she used. It didn't matter if she understood the source of the physical symptoms of pain and suffering. God said, in essence, "I am the healer. It is not up to you. Just ask."

God's message of reassurance brought Nancy great relief and confidence. She no longer worries that her prayers may not sound "professional enough." She is convinced that asking in confidence is the key. Healing is never done by the asker; it is always done by God. She has decided to relax and ask. Although we are insignificant, we are commissioned to ask the One who has the power.

On a Saturday night after the Ruidoso trip, God spoke to Nancy shortly after we had turned out the lights for the night. She "heard" God telling her that He would be in our home the next night and would be healing people. All I knew was that while I was holding her in our bed she started sobbing. She sat up in bed and haltingly asked me, "What would you say if I told you that God just told me He would be here tomorrow night and would be healing people?"

I responded, "I would say we need to announce that at church in the morning and then open our house."

The next morning we approached our pastor about making the announcement. He informed us that his sermon was going to be on healing. He anticipated a prayer time for healing at the end of the service. He was happy to permit us to announce what God had told Nancy.

We were permitted to give our testimonies about the recent healing of Nancy's hands and my back. After the service, several people stood at the front of the church and prayed for those asking for healing. As we prayed, God repeatedly healed people with problems in their hands, backs, knees and feet. The percentage of those healed in our prayer line was so high I wondered if there would be anyone left for healing at our house that evening.

That night twenty four people arrived at our house. I gave a short explanation of why we were there and what we understood God was up to at this time. Then, we all just asked. Nearly everyone there both received prayer and prayed for the others. There were no experts so far as we could tell. We were just people gathered in assurance that God is still in the healing business, business is good and the store is still open.

We witnessed significant healings that night. The praying went on for about four hours. During some of that time, Nancy and I were involved in the laying on of hands. At other times, we were across the room simply agreeing with others who were taking the "laboring oar." I could detect no difference in the reliability of God's response depending on who was praying. He was simply and profoundly pouring out His compassion on His people

Following that night, we started seeking out opportunities to pray for people, both at church services and "as we go." We have found that God's Superstore for Healing and Delivery from Torment knows no geographical limitations. It is not a 'big box' store. No four walls can contain it. Rather, it is a movable feast.

Nancy and I were very "impressed" when we went to Sojourn Church in Carrolton, Texas, to hear Bill Johnson that neither he nor his team which accompanied him did the praying. The praying for healing was done by the un-schooled, uneducated, believers assembled there, praying for strangers in most instances, in prayers lasting less than two minutes. The "experts" were watching and enjoying as God manifested His presence, His power and healing that night.

No series of classes will equip anyone to perform divine healing. It is not the person praying who heals. It is Jesus Himself who heals. That explanation is at the same time simple and profound beyond our ability to understand. We cannot learn the mechanism. We will not learn any magic incantations. We will not discover any secrets that will put God in a box.

We can be absolutely certain that God's objectives and goals remain the same. We can have no such assurance that we understand how He will manifest His power in any particular circumstance to bring His objectives and goals to reality. He doesn't work the same way every time. He doesn't want us to think that He is a puppet and we are the puppet masters. We miss the boat when we expect that God will always act in the same manner.

When we realize it is God who does the healing, we are not as likely to search for someone with a "greater anointing" when presented with a sizable problem. I can't heal a sprained ankle. I also can't heal cancer. Only God can heal anyone of anything. The good news is He is *equally able* to heal both cancer and a sprained ankle. He is *equally willing* to heal both cancer and a sprained ankle. Just ask. Only believe.

What are you waiting for? What are you afraid of? Trust me, you are not big enough to get in God's way when He is pouring out His compassion on His people. If you ask wrong, you need not worry so long as you are asking the One with the power to heal. He doesn't need a consultant. He doesn't need an assistant. He's not wondering what is wrong in the situation. He is not going to withhold His blessing if you command vertebrae to line up if the problem is not with the vertebrae but rather in the muscle.

Quit being so concerned with your reputation. No one truly expects that *you* will heal them.

CHAPTER SIX
Paradigm Shift

There is a new sheriff in town and He brought His kingdom with Him. Jesus brought a paradigm shift.

"The Law and the Prophets were proclaimed until John. Since that time, the good news of the kingdom of God is being preached, and everyone is forcing his way into it." (Luke 16:16) (NIV)

John the Baptist had only one job, to prepare the way for Jesus. The beginning of his public ministry coincided with a dramatic change in emphasis and focus. What we refer to as the Old Testament paled in significance. The realities of the New Testament were being announced and demonstrated.

The emphasis of the Old Testament, the Law and the Prophets, was on the power of sin and the coming Messiah. The Law illustrated both our complete inability to overcome the power of sin and our need for a savior. The Prophets told us how to recognize the Messiah and what he would be like.

Once Jesus was on the scene, He began fulfilling the multiple prophesies concerning the identity and nature of the Messiah.

By the beating and humiliation He endured on the way to the cross and His ultimate death, He paid the price to redeem all of mankind. The voracious appetite of the Law for punishment was satisfied completely. What Jesus accomplished on His way to the cross and on the cross was enough. He will never come again to repeat that process. The payment was made in full.

> *And so he condemned sin in sinful man, in order that the righteous requirements of the law might be fully met in us, who do not live according to the sinful nature but according to the Spirit.* (Romans 8:2-4)

The Law illustrates for us the incredible and undefeatable power of sin. The myriad of rules and the commandments themselves overwhelmed the best intended. While debating the requirements for Gentile believers, Peter referred to the requirements of the Law this way:

> *"Now then, why do you try to test God by putting on the necks of the disciples a yoke that neither we nor our fathers have been able to bear? No! We believe it is through the grace of our Lord Jesus that we are saved, just as they are."* (Acts 15:10-11)

Neither Jesus' Jewish disciples nor the patriarchs were able to bear the yoke of the Law. Yet Jesus came announcing that His yoke is easy. (Matthew 11:30)

Paul recognized the paradigm shift.

> *There is now no condemnation for those who are in Christ Jesus, because through Christ Jesus the law of the Spirit of life set me free from the law of sin and death.* (Romans 8:1)

The *law of sin and death* governed until John. This *law of sin and death* is exactly that yoke that neither the disciples nor the patriarchs were able to bear. After John, the *law of the Spirit of life* was available to believers for the first time. The *Spirit of life* brought freedom from the punishment of the law. That freedom means there is no condemnation for those who are in Christ Jesus.

Power of Sin Prior to The Cross

The Old Testament illustrates the overwhelming power of sin. As an example, in the Old Testament, if an unclean person touches you, you become unclean also. If the unclean person touches your sacrifice, the sacrifice becomes unclean. (Leviticus 5:2-3) In the Old Testament, the "sinful" element polluted the "clean" element. If a leper were to touch someone or the sacrifice, the leper's unclean condition was transferred to the person or the sacrifice.

Power of Sin after Jesus' Resurrection

The New Testament illustrates the power of Jesus' righteousness. Using again the example of a leper, we can examine the report of a leper who approached Jesus, a report contained in several of the Gospels. (Matthew 8:2-4; Mark 1:40-42; Luke 5:12-13) When the leper approached Jesus, he was considered unclean according to the Law and the regulations of the day. If he were to touch Jesus or if Jesus were to touch him, the Law and the regulations would declare Jesus to be unclean.

The leper approached Jesus and said, *"Lord, if you are willing, you can make me clean."* The leper knelt before Jesus before making this statement. He addressed Jesus as Lord. Most astonishing in the context of the time of the event, the leper believed that reliance upon Jesus could make him clean rather than reliance upon the regulations concerning ceremonial cleanness. His actions reflect the power of divine revelation. Long before the "officials" ever considered that perhaps Jesus was the Messiah the leper both knew that Jesus was Lord and was authorized to do something reserved to the priests in the temple.

Jesus' response to the leper is illustrative of the power of Jesus righteousness. Jesus' actions were the opposite of what would have been expected. He reached out and touched the leper.

Jesus then told the leper, "*I am willing. Be clean.*" The Jerusalem Bible translates this passage differently. In the Jerusalem Bible, Jesus said, "*Of course I am willing. Be clean.*" Let there be no doubt of God's will in regard to cleansing the leper. Of course I am willing!

Jesus then cleansed the leper by one of his long, chatty, rambling prayers. He said, "*Be clean.*" The leper was cleansed by the words Jesus spoke.

Jesus dealt with the issue of being clean in John 15:3 when he told his disciples, "*You are already clean because of the word I have spoken to you.*" The Greek word translated clean in both the instance of the leper and the disciples derives from *katharos* which means clean, clear or pure. Since the same Greek word is used in both instances, Jesus is dealing with the same issue, the purity of the person.

The disciples did not have leprosy. Jesus was not making them ceremonially clean under the Jewish regulations. He made them clean even when they weren't sick.

The leper was being made more than ceremonially clean. He was cured of his leprosy. His physical illness was dealt with by Jesus word every bit as much as his status in the temple.

There are other examples of Jesus dealing with sickness or disability at the same time he dealt with status in the kingdom.

When the friends lowered the paralytic through the roof, Jesus said to him, *"Friend, your sins are forgiven."* (Luke 5:20)

Realizing that the religious folks of the day were questioning in their hearts His authority to forgive sins, Jesus said, *"Which is easier: to say, 'Your sins are forgiven,' or to say, 'Get up and walk'"?* (Luke 5:23) Jesus seems to be suggesting that physical healing and forgiveness of sin are equally available from Him. His choice of words was a matter of convenience, "Which is easier?"

Then Jesus did something astonishing. Looking at the religious folks of the day He said, *"But that you may know that the Son of Man has authority on earth to forgive sins . . . ."* (Luke 5:24) The sentence is left mid-idea. He then turned to the paralytic and said, *"I tell you, get up, take your mat and go home."* (Luke 5:24) Jesus proved his authority to forgive sins by healing the paralytic with his words. Jesus knew that both forgiveness of sins and healing were available through the same power and authority.

Jesus had already forgiven his sins. (Luke 5:20) Now his body was healed.

Why Jesus Came to Earth

While our mind was being renewed, as we were changing our way of thinking, Nancy and I studied why God sent Jesus to earth. The Bible reports at least five purposes:

o   to save His people from their sins (Matthew 1:20-21);
o   to destroy the works of the devil (1 John 3:8);
o   to bring life to the full (John 10:10);
o   to seek and save what was lost (Luke 19:1-10); and
o   to preach the good news (Luke 4:43).

What Does It Mean to Be "Saved"?

In Joseph's angelic visitation, the angel of the Lord explained to him that Mary would give birth to a son who was to be named Jesus because *"He will save His people from their sins."* (Matthew 1:21)

Salvation is a package deal. The Greek word translated *salvation* in the New Testament is *soteria*, which derives from the Greek word *sozo*. *Sozo* is a complete restoration of body, soul and spirit. This complete restoration of body, soul and spirit is all part of the atonement. (Isaiah 53:4-6)

The result of restoration of my *spirit* is that my eternal destination is changed from hell to heaven. This is the part of salvation most emphasized in the church today. If that were all that salvation meant, it is well worth it. However, there is so much more.

Sozo also includes restoration of the *body* (physical healing) and the *soul* (healing of the mind and emotions). Salvation in the kingdom is so much larger than we have been taught. Salvation is so huge. Don't leave home without it.

The name "Jesus" means "Yahweh is our salvation." The very name of Jesus reminds us that God has provided our complete restoration of body, soul and spirit to the same status mankind enjoyed before the fall. What are the hallmarks of Mankind's status before the fall? To what have we been restored?

Before the fall,

o   Man was created in God's own image which means that he was not sick, not subject to torment, at peace with God and not controlled by a sinful nature;

o   God had breathed His Spirit into him, filling him with life;

o Man was completely dependent upon God for the knowledge of good and evil; and

o Man stood unashamed in daily communion with God.

Jesus restored us to "our" prior condition. He rescued us from the dominion of darkness. God brought us into the kingdom of the Son He loves, in whom we have redemption. Jesus' death reconciled us to God to present us holy in His sight, without blemish and free from accusation. (Colossians 1: 13-22)

Now, that's what I am talking about!

To Destroy the Works of the Devil

The Apostle John put it this way: *"For this purpose the Son of God was manifested, that he might destroy the works of the devil."* (1 John 3:8) Jesus did not engage in warfare with the devil as a side-line business. This battle was the main event.

The works of the devil include sin, sickness, torment and death. In many circles, our behavior and its effects on our eternal destination are the main focus while physical and emotional healing is relegated to "side-show" status. Are you concerned primarily with cleaning up your act in order to become more acceptable to God? Where in your daily walk are you exhibiting a focus on delivering God's compassion to His people?

None of the works of the devil are present in heaven. Heaven knows no sin, no sickness, no torment and no death. No wonder they call it heaven!

All sin, all sickness, all torment and all spiritual death are from the devil. Since the source of these works is the devil, God does not ever use them to discipline His children. He did not send Jesus to destroy anything He was going to use. I am not saying God will not work in the midst of an attack by the devil. I am saying that God is not the author of the works of the devil and does not use them to punish or discipline His people.

If Jesus was manifested to destroy the works of the devil, we can be certain that God is unalterably opposed to sin, sickness, torment and death. Jesus is the exact representation of the Father. (Hebrews 1:3) If you want to know the Father's will on any issue, look at what Jesus did. His actions reveal the Father's will. Jesus never turned His back on sickness, torment or spiritual death. Jesus never left sickness or torment unaddressed. Jesus went around healing all who were oppressed by the devil. (Acts 10:38)

Jesus was manifested to destroy the works of the devil. (1 John 3:8) The last words of Jesus on the cross were: "It is finished." (John 19:30) He did not mean that His life was finished. It was not. Rather, He was announcing that He had finished the work He came to do.

One result of the devil's defeat is that Jesus "*has made perfect forever those who are being made holy by his one sacrifice.*" (Hebrews 10:14) I am made perfect in my spirit because of what Jesus did, not *because* of any of my actions but rather *in spite of* my actions. I am progressively being made holy by the transformation which results from the renewing of my mind. (Romans 12:2)

Since I have already been made perfect, and my sanctification continues as my mind continues to be renewed, I should spend precious little time "navel gazing." I have no power or ability to clean up my act sufficiently to enter heaven on my own merits. I can get there solely through what Jesus has already accomplished.

Rather than navel gazing, I should be seeking to co-labor with God in accomplishing His purposes in the kingdom. Paul describes us as "*workers together with Him*" or "*God's fellow workers.*" (2 Corinthians 6:1 KJV and NIV respectively.) The work of God is two-fold, the spread of the kingdom to new believers and the delivery of God's compassion to those who are in any way afflicted by the devil.

Life to the Full

The aim of salvation is not to enable us to live without sin. Rather, the aim of salvation is the restoration of life.

Jesus explained to the Pharisees: "*The thief comes only to steal and kill and destroy; I have come that they may have life, and have it to the full. I am the good shepherd. The good shepherd lays down his life for the sheep.*" (John 10:10-11) The abundant life Jesus promised results from a complete restoration of body, soul and spirit. This is life to the full. We can receive that life only because our good shepherd laid down His life for us, His sheep.

The thief came to steal, kill and destroy. The devil is a created being, more crafty than any of the wild animals the LORD God had made. (Genesis 3:1) I need to be aware of his craftiness. He uses this craftiness to attack me where I am weakest.

If my knowledge, understanding and appreciation of my relationship to God is weak, I should expect him to try to exploit that weakness. If my knowledge of what God has said is weak, I should expect him to try to exploit that weakness. When I am strong in my knowledge of God's Word and secure in my relationship to the Father in the kingdom, the devil's attacks are easily discerned and avoided. It is when I am weak (all too often) that I am vulnerable to attack.

The serpent encouraged the woman to question the word of God. He approached the woman, in part, because her knowledge of what God had said was second hand. The serpent asked, "*Did God really say . . . .*" The devil questioned God's reliability by questioning the reliability of the source of her information. The only way she would know what God said was to rely on what the man said that God said. Once the source was changed from God to the man, the battle was now being fought on different ground. Once the source was the man, the truth of what he had reported as a conversation from God could be assailed.

The woman knew for certain that Adam had *reported to her* that she was not to eat of the fruit of the tree of the knowledge of good and evil or she would surely die. This must have seemed like a harsh pronouncement from a God she knew to be a caring, loving, provider, comforter and friend.

So, what did the serpent do? He suggested a reason why God couldn't have said what he said. He provided her *intellect* a way to doubt the accuracy of what she had heard from Adam and a reason why she should not comply. At the devil's suggestion, she saw that the fruit was good for food, pleasing to the eye, and desirable for gaining wisdom. With all these pluses, how could it be that God had said if she ate fruit from this tree that she would surely die? The woman's intellectual inability to understand the wisdom of the one and only command she had received prevented her from relying on the providence of God gained through absolute trust in the truth of His Word. The serpent used her shortcoming and limited understanding as the key to steal, kill and destroy.

Make no mistake. God had told Adam that he would surely die if he ate the fruit from the tree in the center of the garden. Although the devil got the woman to question whether God had said that, and if He had, did He mean it, the truth was that eating that fruit would lead to death.

God said death was the consequence of eating of the fruit from the tree of the knowledge of good and evil. Eve and then Adam ate it. Their physical bodies did not die for over 800 years following this encounter. Is God a liar? Did Moses get this part wrong? Choose! Either God is a liar, in which case we need not bother with the rest of the book, or the woman and the man died—not 800 plus years later—right then.

The death experienced by the man and the woman was spiritual death, not physical death. Spiritual death includes loss of being created in the image and likeness of God. No longer were the man and the woman to be free from sickness, disease and torment. No longer were they to be able to live a spirit controlled life. A life controlled by a sin nature began.

Although Adam was created in God's image, Adam's children were created "in his own likeness, in his own image." (Genesis 5:1-4) When these children were born, the man and the woman were already spiritually dead. Adam's children, born in his likeness and image, were born spiritually dead. All of us born since the fall are born spiritually dead and in need of *sozo*, the complete restoration of body, soul and spirit.

God expelled the man and the woman from the garden. He posted a cherubim and a flaming sword flashing back and forth to guard the way to the tree of life." (Genesis 3:24) Only if the man and woman were spiritually dead would it be necessary to guard the way to the tree of life.

What mankind needs is restoration of the spiritual life lost at the time of the fall. Jesus provided that restoration:

> *For just as the Father raises the dead and gives them life, even so the Son gives life to whom he is pleased to give it . . . . "I tell you the truth, whoever hears my word and believes him who sent me has eternal life and will not be condemned; he has crossed over from death to life. I tell you the truth, a time is coming and has now come when the dead will hear the voice of the Son of God and those who hear will live.* (John 5:21-25)

Jesus died to fulfill the sacrificial requirement of the law for the forgiveness of sins. The shedding of blood in the perfect sacrifice was completed on Friday. What about Sunday? Jesus rose on Sunday and lives forever to give us life in Him.

Unbelief is the sin which can keep us separated from God.

> *"For God did not send his Son into the world to condemn the world, but to save the world through him. Whoever believes in him is not condemned, but whoever does not believe stands condemned already because he has not believed in the name of God's one and only Son."* (John 3:17-18)

Unless we believe in Jesus, we already are condemned. We need not do one more thing to go to hell. No acts of disobedience are required. No bad thoughts or attitudes are necessary. We are already condemned.

Paul recognized the fruit of the restoration of life:

> *"Therefore, there is now no condemnation for those who are in Christ Jesus, because through Christ Jesus the law of the Spirit of life set me free from the law of sin and death."* (Romans 8:1-2)

Under the law of sin and death, the wages of sin is death. However, under the law of the Spirit of life, the gift of God is eternal life in Christ Jesus our Lord. (Romans 6:23) Death is a **payment.** Eternal life is a **gift.**

Jesus came to give us back the life which the liar had stolen and destroyed. The really good news is that the life He came to give us is life to the full, the abundant life. This abundant life includes not only forgiveness of sin but also physical healing and delivery from torment.

New Life

Both John the Baptist and Jesus proclaimed that "the kingdom of heaven is near" (Matthew 3:2; 4:17) or the "kingdom of God is near" (Mark 1:14). They both announced a new life available to believers:

John: *"Whoever believes in the Son has eternal life, but whoever rejects the Son will not see life, for God's wrath remains on him."* (John 3:36)

Jesus: *"I tell you the truth, whoever hears my word and believes him who sent me has eternal life and will not be condemned; he has crossed over from death to life."* (John 5:24)

For God so loved the world that he gave his one and only Son, that whoever believes in him shall not perish but have eternal life. For God did not send his Son into the world to condemn the world, but to save the world through him. Whoever believes in him is not condemned, but whoever does not believe stands condemned already because he has not believed in the name of God's one and only Son." (John 3:16-18)

Our status in the kingdom of God is clear. Until we believe in Jesus, we are dead in our sins. God's wrath remains on us. We enter the kingdom, crossing over from death to life, by hearing Jesus' words and believing the one who sent Him.

We do not enter the kingdom of God equipped to never sin again. In the kingdom, our righteousness is not dependent upon living a sinless life. Rather, we are equipped to become alive and live the abundant life Jesus brought with Him.

Yet to all who received him, to those who believed in his name, he gave the right to become children

> *of God—children born not of natural descent, nor*
> *of human decision or a husband's will, but born of*
> *God.* (John 1:12-13)

When I entered the kingdom of God, I:

o   was born from above;
o   became free from the law of sin and death; and
o   am no longer subject to condemnation.

When I entered the kingdom of God, I became the beneficiary of an enormous promise:

> *"I tell you the truth, anyone who has faith in me will*
> *do what I have been doing. He will do even greater*
> *things than these, because I am going to the Father.*
> *And I will do whatever you ask in my name, so that*
> *the Son may bring glory to the Father. You may*
> *ask me for anything in my name, and I will do it."*
> (John 14:12-14)

Under the Law and the Prophets, it was not our job to co-labor with God in miracles, signs and wonders. We had neither authority to act or the ability to access the power to participate in the miracles, signs and wonders God was doing.

In the kingdom of God, we are commissioned to co-labor with God in accomplishing His purposes. In order to equip us for that labor, we have been given both the authority to act and access to the power necessary. Understanding the paradigm shift described in this chapter greatly assists in participation with God in delivering His compassion to His people.

The backing of heaven is required for me to be a co-laborer with God. (1 Corinthians 3:9) God did not risk His reputation by charging me to do something without giving me both the authority to act on His behalf and access to the power necessary to accomplish His purposes.

New Status

My status in the kingdom is considerably different from my status as revealed in the Law and the Prophets. Accepting my new status in the kingdom is an important step in the renewing of my mind.

The consequence and significance of my behavior is substantially different in the kingdom. Consequently, my focus should not be upon my behavior and the consequences of that behavior. Rather, my focus should recognize all of the benefits which have been bestowed on me in the kingdom.

A renewed mind will fully appreciate the kingdom realities summarized below.

<u>I am a new creation, created to do good works.</u>

- o If anyone is in Christ, he is a new creation; the old has gone, the new has come. (2 Cor. 5:17)
- o We are God's workmanship, created in Christ Jesus to do good works, which God prepared in advance for us to do. (Ephesians 2:10)
- o The blood of Christ, cleansed our consciences from acts that lead to death, so that we may serve the living God. (Hebrews 9:14)

<u>I am free from the power of sin.</u>

- o Sin shall not be your master, because you are not under law, but under grace. **You have been set free from sin** and have become slaves to righteousness. (Romans 6:14-18) o Christ is the mediator of a new covenant now that He has died as a ransom to **set us free from the sins** committed under the first covenant. (Hebrews 9:15)

o We are no longer under the supervision of the law. (Galatians 3:25)

God does not count my sins against me any longer.

o God reconciled the world to Himself in Christ, not counting men's sins against them. (2 Cor. 5:19)

o God forgives my wickedness and will remember my sins no more. (Hebrews 8:12)

o Their sins and lawless acts God will remember no more. Where these have been forgiven, there is no longer any sacrifice for sin. (Hebrews 10:17-18)

I have been made the righteousness of God.

o God made him who had no sin to be sin for us, so that in him we might become the righteousness of God. (2 Cor. 5:21)

o By one sacrifice Jesus made perfect forever those who are being made holy. (Hebrews 10:14)

Jesus acted once for all.

o Jesus was sacrificed for our sins once for all when he offered himself. (Hebrews 7:27)

o Jesus appeared once for all at the end of the ages to do away with sin by the sacrifice of himself. Christ was sacrificed once to take away the sins of many people. (Hebrews 9:25-28)

o We have been made holy through the sacrifice of the body of Jesus Christ once for all. (Hebrews 10:10).

The kingdom of God is not primarily concerned with behavior.

o   For the kingdom of God is not a matter of eating and
    drinking, but of righteousness, peace and joy in the
    Holy Spirit. (Romans 14:17)

CHAPTER SEVEN

Are You In or Out?

God has always offered a choice.

> *"See, I set before you today life and prosperity, death and destruction . . . . This day I call heaven and earth as witnesses against you that I have set before you life and death, blessings and curses. Now choose life, so that you and your children may live and that you may love the LORD your God, listen to his voice, and hold fast to him."* (Deuteronomy 30:15-20)

There are two competing voices, Jesus' and the liar's. The renewing of your mind requires that you choose which one you will believe. Will you believe that you are a miserable sinner and completely worthless to God in ministry? Do you believe your status disqualifies you from a life of miracles, signs and wonders? Will your renewed mind grasp and completely accept that your relationship to God qualifies you uniquely for just exactly that?

In order to believe you are disqualified, you must call God a liar. The choice is ours. Our status in the kingdom is clear Because He Said So. The liar has no power to change the Word of God.

Our service to God is made possible by the cleansing of Jesus' blood. He cleaned us up for ministry. When we become alive in Jesus, we are a new creation which is designed to do good works. The good works are not the things we imagine. Rather, they are the good works that God has prepared in advance for us to do. God has prepared good works for us to perform while we are yoked together with Jesus, whose yoke is easy and whose burden is light. (Matthew 11:30)

Protect Your Seed

I am qualified to participate in miracles, signs and wonders because of the status conferred on me by what Jesus did. *"By one sacrifice Jesus has made perfect forever those who are being made holy."* (Hebrews 10:14) While the process of sanctification will continue throughout my life, my status in the kingdom is that God has already made me perfect forever. The status He has conferred upon me cannot be changed by my shortcomings. Remember, the woman who wiped Jesus' feet with her tears and poured perfume on Him while He visited the Pharisee's house was a notorious sinner. However, she left that night smelling just like Jesus. (Luke 7:36-39)

It is easy for me to forget that all the power of a stately oak tree was once contained in a little acorn. We see so many acorns which amount to nothing. Each acorns destiny or potential, if properly protected, is to become the full tree. The difference between an acorn which is crushed under my foot and an oak tree depends upon where that acorn fell.

In the parable of the farmer and his seed, Jesus explained the different potentials for the seed depending upon the point of planting. (Matthew 13:3-9; Mark 4:3-8; and Luke 8:5-8) The seed that fell among the thorns was choked out by the thorns. The seed that fell on good soil produced a good crop.

In the parable of the weeds, Jesus further explained the problem with weeds. (Matthew 13:24-30) In that parable, Jesus makes it clear that the weeds will be permitted to grow with the wheat until the harvest. All of the ground used by the weeds is not available to the wheat.

Focusing on our behavior while forgetting our new status in the kingdom has a choking effect on the seed planted in our soil. The more thorns and weeds we have in our garden, the smaller the wheat crop. The wheat seed will become wheat in both instances. However, there will not be as great a harvest because the thorns or weeds take away nutrients to the discouragement of the wheat.

When my focus is on cleaning up my act, I can scarcely take my eyes off of myself long enough to discern what the Father is doing in delivering his compassion to those around me. Not only will I not know what He is doing, I will have neither the time nor the desire to participate. I will be exhausted trying to improve my flesh. Surely if I was able to improve my flesh by my own effort, Jesus did not need to come to usher me into the kingdom.

When my renewed mind understands my status in the kingdom, I realize that I stand in the same relationship to the Father as Jesus did. I am righteous because of what He did. I need not let my sins get in my way since He is not counting them against me. I have access to the power of the Holy Spirit through Baptism in the Holy Spirit.

In this garden, the acorn will become the oak tree which continues to produce more acorns throughout its life.

Not Disqualified by Actions

Some avoid participation in miracles, signs and wonders out of a sense of unworthiness. They simply are too aware of past and current sins. They believe that a sense of humility should cause them to self-disqualify from participation. "Surely God won't use me. Look what I have done."

This attitude is a false sense of humility. The attitude can be stated, "I am a humble person. I would never presume that God would use the likes of me to accomplish His purposes."

The problem with this attitude is that it conflicts directly with the Word of God. How dare we deny that we are exactly what the Word says we are, the righteousness of God whose sins God remembers no more, empowered by the Holy Spirit to co-labor with God?

For Ministry.

An awareness of current or past sins seldom inhibits believers from cooking for the church supper, cleaning up after functions, feeding the hungry, or caring for children during adult activities. There is a tendency to seek out good works that can be done under our own power. If a ministry does not require God to "show up" then that ministry can be performed with equal results by any service organization. The Church is not another service organization operating under its own power.

Fewer people choose to participate in ministries when accomplishment of the ministry goal requires God to act. The attitude seems to be that if God is required, He won't show up if a sinner is present. This is totally the opposite of what Jesus said. Jesus "hung out" with sinners. He came to save sinners, not the "righteous." (Matthew 9:12-13; Mark 2:16-17; Luke 5:30-32)

Because He Said So (Second Edition)

Sin awareness requires an accuser. It is not coincidental that the name *satan* means "accuser." One of his main ploys is to point out our inability to conform our conduct to the law, thereby creating guilt, humiliation and shame.

The good news is that the accuser has been cast down. Michael and the angels fought with the accuser who was found to be too weak. He lost his place in heaven and was hurled down to earth.

> *"Now have come the salvation and the power and the kingdom of our God, and the authority of his Christ. For the accuser of our brothers, who accuses them before our God day and night, has been hurled down. They overcame him by the blood of the Lamb and by the word of their testimony; they did not love their lives so much as to shrink from death."* (Revelation 12:10-11)

The accuser has no truth in him. *"When he lies, he speaks his native language, for he is a liar and the father of lies."* (John 8:44) A lie can only imprison someone if the lie is believed. The liar is empowered every time we believe a lie.

On the other hand, Jesus is the truth and the truth sets us free. (John 8:32) My future in the kingdom is free from my bad actions.

The Apostle Paul is an excellent example of the truth that past bad actions do not disqualify a believer from ministry in the present and in the future. Paul breathed *"out murderous threats against the Lord's disciples. He went to the high priest and asked him for letters to the synagogues in Damascus, so that if he found any there who belonged to the Way, whether men or women, he might take them as prisoners to Jerusalem."* (Acts 9:1-2) Paul was "a blasphemer and a persecutor and a violent man." (1 Timothy 1:13) He stood

97

by in approval at the stoning of Stephen. (Acts 8:1) He described himself as the chief sinner. (1 Timothy 1:15)

Paul experienced a prolonged period of unbelief. No matter how long the past period of unbelief, the only relevant time period in the kingdom is now. The very second you become a believer the years, even eons, of unbelief disappear in the twinkling of an eye. It doesn't matter how long you may have believed that God was no longer in the healing business. It doesn't matter how long you may have believed that miracles, signs and wonders passed away with the canonization of the New Testament or the passing of the apostolic age. As soon as those beliefs are set aside, the past record of unbelief no longer matters.

Now compared to Paul's history, what have you done that is so bad? You are just as forgiven as Paul. Your past is simply irrelevant to your present and your future ministry opportunities. It is impossible for you to have been worse than Paul in the context of unbelief. He not only did not believe in Jesus as the Messiah, he wanted to kill any who did believe. How can you think you surpass him?

Paul didn't do so well following his conversion either. He was unable to act in a way that would satisfy the requirements of the law.

> "I do not understand what I do. For what I want to do I do not do, but what I hate I do. And if I do what I do not want to do, I agree that the law is good. As it is, it is no longer I myself who do it, but it is sin living in me. I know that nothing good lives in me, that is, in my sinful nature. For I have the desire to do what is good, but I cannot carry it out. For what I do is not the good I want to do; no, the evil I do not want to do—this I keep on doing." (Romans 7:15-19)

Paul was thoroughly disgusted with himself. *"What a wretched man I am! Who will rescue me from this body of death?"* (Romans 7:24) The devil wants us to forget that we are in the same boat with Paul. He wants us to not be fellow workers with God, as Paul was. If the devil can keep us out of the game, others will be impacted.

Every church board, every great and mighty ministry existing since the death and resurrection of Jesus Christ is populated one hundred percent with people who keep on doing evil, just like Paul. It is pride in our sin that makes us feel that we are worse than Paul, not worthy to co-labor with God. What can be worse conduct than to keep on doing the evil that you do not want to do? Yet, that is exactly what Paul did.

False humility causes believers to exalt their bad behavior as a disqualifying factor. Their sin awareness makes them want to crucify themselves. To those believers, I say, "Get off the cross, we need the wood." Since *"there is now no condemnation for those who are in Christ Jesus"* (Romans 8:1), get over it and get busy.

For Receiving Healing.

God heals His people because He is good, not because they are good. He heals as a manifestation of His love, not as a reward for good behavior. He heals because He is worthy of glory, honor and praise, not because His people are worthy.

The sin awareness problem also prevents many from seeking healing or delivery from torment. Just as in the ministry context, the attitude seems to be that God would not choose to heal me or deliver me from torment because of my attitudes or actions, either in the present or in the past.

The prior sections of this chapter are equally applicable to the person who seeks healing or delivery from torment as it is applicable to those who would be praying for that person. Whether involved in ministry or seeking the compassion of God, the born again believer's status is the same.

Some men came to Jesus to seek healing for a paralytic. They lowered the paralytic through the roof on his mat. Jesus saw the faith of those bringing the paralytic and said to the paralytic, *"Friend, your sins are forgiven."* After some discussion with the Pharisees and teachers of the law, Jesus demonstrated his authority to announce forgiveness of sin by commanding the paralytic to *"get up, take your mat and go home."* (Luke 4:18-24)

Jesus did not:

o condition the paralytic's healing on a particular attitude or thought pattern;

o command the paralytic to repent;

o question whether the paralytic wanted a saving relationship with the Son of God;

o send the paralytic off to fast and pray for a period of time to become worthy of healing;

o seek a promise of changed behavior; or

o require a sacrifice at the temple.

Rather, Jesus simply announced that the paralytic's sins were forgiven.

Jesus knew that *"the power of the Lord was present for him to heal the sick."* (Luke 5:17) He knew from His prayers with the Father that the Father was healing His people in that place. He knew that God was delivering His compassion to His people irrespective of their compliance or non-compliance with the sacrificial system in place for the forgiveness of sins. In short, Jesus knew the Father had not withheld His power to heal the sick in any instance recorded in the scriptures based upon a sin-condition. Since Jesus only said what He heard the Father saying, He had already heard the Father say the paralytic's sins were forgiven.

Jesus represented the Father *exactly* in all that He did. Jesus "*is the radiance of God's glory and the exact representation of His being, sustaining all things by His powerful word.*" (Hebrews 1:3) If I want to know what the Father's will is, all I need to do is look at what Jesus did in the same or similar circumstance.

Jesus healed **all** the people who came to Him seeking healing. He delivered **all** the people from torment who came to Him seeking deliverance. Since Jesus never conditioned healing or deliverance on proper standing in the sacrificial system, we know that the Father imposed no such limitation on the delivery of His compassion to His people.

CHAPTER EIGHT

The Testimony of Jesus
The Spirit of Prophecy

In one of the most pregnant verses in the Bible an angel announced to John, *"The testimony of Jesus is the spirit of prophecy."* (Revelation 19:10)

For more than two years a group met at our house on Sunday evenings to consider miracles, signs and wonders and then gather in prayer for each other. During that period we started paying attention to whether we could sense the presence of God in the room. We knew intellectually He was there because He has promised never to leave us or forsake us. (Joshua 1:5; Hebrews 13:5) We knew He promised to be with us always to the very end. (Matthew 28:20) But, we were trying to discern his presence experientially. We wanted to know He was present rather than believe He was present.

When someone in the group discerned the presence of God, he would say, "He is here right now." Many others often agreed that they could also sense God's presence. As we discussed how we knew He was present, we learned that each person experienced God's presence in a different way. Some aspects might overlap from person to person but there were also individual differences. Some had goose bumps, some felt an energy in the room, some had oil and gold sparkles on their hands. We learned that it is a real confidence builder to experience God's presence when trying to partner with Him.

On those occasions, which happened each Sunday, we would pause and pray for any needs immediately. We weren't sure just exactly what was going on but we knew that when we sensed God's presence, His power was also present to heal our physical bodies, our minds and emotions.

For many months when anyone would say, "the testimony of Jesus is the spirit of prophecy," many in the room would be announcing "He is here." Merely speaking the words seemed to usher in a fullness of sensations which made His presence more real. The atmosphere clearly changed.

Prophecy is God talking through human servants. The prophet adds nothing to the word of God. He simply says what he has heard or seen. The word of God is the most powerful force in the universe. He spoke the world into being. His word accomplishes its purposes and never returns to Him void. (Isaiah 55:11)

The testimony of Jesus includes a recitation of all He did while He walked the earth, all He said, what He has done following His resurrection in days gone by and what He is doing currently in our lives. When we tell the stories of healing, we are giving the testimony of Jesus. The recitation of what we have seen Jesus accomplish changes the atmosphere. It is often accompanied by the physical sensing of God's presence.

Nancy and I realized relatively early on that we were more comfortable in praying for people in non-church settings if we gave the testimony of Jesus before praying. We experienced a ridiculously high percentage of people who God healed in "non-traditional" venues. Those healings then became part of the testimony of Jesus.

From Belief to Knowing

It was he who gave some to be apostles, some to be prophets, some to be evangelists, and some to be pastors and teachers, to prepare God's people for works of service, so that the body of Christ may be built up until we all reach unity in the faith and in the knowledge of the Son of God and become mature, attaining to the whole measure of the fullness of Christ. Then we will no longer be infants, tossed back and forth by the waves, and blown here and there by every wind of teaching and by the cunning and craftiness of men in their deceitful scheming. Instead, speaking the truth in love, we will in all things grow up into him who is the Head, that is, Christ. (Ephesians 4:11-15)

One of the aspects of the journey to a renewed mind is a transition from *believing* in God to *knowing* Him. God appoints members of the Body of Christ to perform different functions which have as their aim the preparation of the people of God for works of service. The goal of these works of service is to build up the Body of Christ into maturity of the Body. In this maturity, the Body will experience unity in the faith, unity in the knowledge of Christ leading to attaining the measure of the fullness of Christ. We will no longer be tossed back and forth by the winds and the waves of different teachings but rather will know God for ourselves.

As part of the testimony of Jesus, God gave us confidence builders to encourage us in the journey from believing in Him to knowing Him. As we saw God heal more and more people of more and more complex issues, we had both the thrill of knowing that God had changed the history of the person He healed and the increasing certainty that the God of our hopes, wishes and desires was not only real but was intimately concerned with the everyday problems of His people.

Before beginning this journey I viewed those who experienced displays of miracles, signs and wonders as specially gifted by God. I felt about them the same way Butch Cassidy and the Sundance Kid marveled at the professional trackers the railroad sent to capture them. In the 1970 movie, *Butch Cassidy and the Sundance Kid,* Butch and Sundance use their best tricks to lose the men who are tracking them. None of their tricks are successful to throw off the trackers. As they look back in amazement at the trackers, Butch and Sundance often have this exchange, which captures my original thoughts about healing.

> "I can't do that. Can you do that? How do they
> do that? Who are those guys?"

You should expect to become one of "those guys" as your mind is being renewed and you change your way of thinking. Take Jesus at His word and see what happens all around you.

Confidence Builders

Lynda was the first confidence builder. Words of knowledge and words of wisdom about Lynda's business gave us increasing confidence that God had Lynda in His cross-hairs. The Holy Spirit had his eye on her, without question. While the words of knowledge and wisdom were encouraging to us, when she could raise her left arm without pain we were in awe of God's power and His love for His people. We told anyone who would listen.

God not only had His eye on Lynda, He was watching her entire family. Lynda's youngest daughter, Rachelle, stepped off a step and severely sprained her right ankle. By the time we saw her, Rachelle had been on crutches a few days. She was still unable to put any weight on her right foot and was in considerable pain.

One evening Lynda had a business meeting with her company. After the meeting, Lynda and Rachelle came to our house to report on the business meeting. We had overnight guests who were watching TV on the first floor of our home. My office was on the second floor, up twenty steps in a stairway with three turns. Rachelle "crutched" her way up the stairs and sat with us while Lynda gave the report on her business meeting.

When the business was done, we asked Rachelle about her ankle. She reported she had an appointment the following morning to request a rolling support of some sort for her to use in getting around at work. She was unable to put any weight on that ankle.

Lynda asked her, "Rachelle, do you believe that God can heal your ankle? You saw what He has done for my shoulder."

Rachelle's response was typical. "Sure, I believe He *can* heal it."

Lynda said, "But do you believe He *will*?

Rachelle responded, "I am not so sure about that."

We talked with Rachelle for awhile trying to convince her that God was willing to heal her just as He had healed her mom. After a few minutes, we asked her to put her leg up on a chair we positioned in front of her. Nancy, Lynda and I prayed a short prayer for Rachelle. Then we asked her to "check it out" by standing up and walking across the room.

She was quite reluctant to give it a try. She knew all too well the pain she would feel if she tried to put any weight on that right foot. Haltingly, she put weight on her right foot and then "limped" across the room. This limping gait was a miracle to us. She was able to put weight on that foot and walk with moderate pain.

We explained that when Jesus prayed for a blind man who then saw men as trees walking, Jesus' next step was to pray again. (Mark 8:22-25) We sat her down and prayed again, this time even shorter than the first time. We then instructed her to check it out.

This time, she rose from the chair and walked across the room with no limp and no pain. While Nancy and I tried to look calm on the outside, inside we were both thinking, "Oh, my God, You have done it again!" I knew I couldn't do that. I was pretty sure Nancy couldn't do that. We knew full well *who* had done it.

As Rachelle stood looking us, an expression of amazement on her face, her right hip looked like it was higher than her left. I asked if her hip hurt.

Lynda said, "She has scoliosis in her back. She always stands that way. Rachelle, turn around so we can see your pockets."

Rachelle turned around and faced away from us. The pockets on her jeans showed the effect of the scoliosis clearly. The right pocket was higher than the left.

We had Rachelle sit down again and prayed about the scoliosis. We then had her check it out again. She walked across the room and back. When she turned away from us after this trip across the room, her pockets lined up perfectly.

Lynda was nearly beside herself. She had just seen God heal the sprained ankle and then realign Rachelle's spine so she could stand straight. We joined in her rejoicing.

It was time for them to go home. Rachelle walked down the twenty steps without using the banister and with no limp. I carried her crutches for her. When she got to the bottom of the stairs she walked into the living room, spoke to our company and then walked, without pain and no limp, out to the car.

The next day she kept her appointment with the doctor. After she explained to him what had happened, he told her she should be careful and not run any marathons! This was the visit scheduled for her to receive some sort of scooter device to enable her to get around at work. No need for a scooter any longer!

Nancy and I were now officially encouraged. It was time to bring this experience to our church.

Shortly after Rachelle's experience we attended a Friday night worship service at our home church. During the worship God impressed on me that He was willing to heal Linda (not Lynda) of a problem she had resulting from complications of a hip replacement surgery that left her left leg shorter than her right leg.

I approached Linda and said, "I believe God is willing to heal your hip problem. Would it be alright if I get a group together to pray for you?"

Linda gave her OK. I asked her to go the side of the sanctuary while I gathered up some folks. One of those folks, Janice, was busy doing something for a minute or two and came late to the prayer session. We were already praying for Linda. She was seated in a chair with her legs up on another chair placed in front of her. It was clear that her left leg was shorter than her right leg. Janice put her hands on Linda's left ankle and foot without knowing what we were praying for.

After a short time of prayer, we asked Linda to check it out. We had all seen that her legs were now the same length as they rested on the chair. She stood up and found she had no pain in that left leg.

I left for a moment and told another woman we were going to pray for that we would be right with her. When I returned to the group around Linda she was standing on one leg with the other drawn up behind her, like a flamingo. I asked, "What are you doing?"

She said, "I can't do this. When I put my clothes on, if I try to stand on one leg, I fall down."

I said, "It seems you are doing it now!" All involved were standing in awe of what God had done. No one had any question over who had done the healing.

Janice came to me and said, "I got here late. What were we praying for?"

I explained about the left leg being too short because of the surgery.

Janice asked, "What does it feel like when a leg grows?"

I replied, "I have no idea. I have never seen this before."

Janice said, "I felt her left ankle and foot jerk three times. I just wondered if that is the way it is supposed to feel?"

On Sunday I approached Linda and said, "Give me a good report."

She replied, "You know, I haven't been able to wear heels since the surgery. Look!"

I looked at her feet and there she was on high heels. God is just awesome.

During the service that day, the pastor invited people who needed prayer to raise their hands and requested those around them to pray for them. Mary was in the row behind us, visiting from California. She raised her hand. I was the only person who was available to pray for her as the others in my row had gone to pray for others. I was immediately beset by the knowledge that "I can't do that." I was stuck praying by myself. What now?

I gave her my best prayer for her sore back and asked her to check it out. Her back was still sore. I started to explain about the blind man who saw men as trees walking when she said, "My back is sore because one of my legs is shorter than the other."

I said, "Wait right here."

I ran about ten rows forward and grabbed Linda. I explained what was going on and she agreed to come with me.

Linda told Mary what God had done for her on Friday and showed her the high heels. We then prayed for Mary again. After this prayer, she checked it out again.

She reported, "I have no pain."

We sat her down and measured her legs. They were the same length.

Mary was visiting Granbury for a short time from California. Nancy ran into her at Kroger on the following Tuesday and asked how she was.

She reported no pain whatsoever.

There were now an expanding number of people who were officially excited.

Lynda was among those who were officially excited. She called one day to ask Nancy and me to join her at Chili's for lunch. When we arrived we found Lynda with a long-time friend of hers, Diane. We noticed that Diane had a real cute, multi-colored cane but didn't discuss it during lunch.

The lunch was awful. Linda and Diane seemed to be at odds. Nancy and I were wondering why we got to be participants in this meal. Near the end of the meal Lynda explained that Diane had experienced a bad result in a hip replacement surgery and wondered if we could pray for her.

I begged off praying for Diane at Chili's. I suggested we adjourn to my office, about a block away. When we got there, Nancy and I watched Diane walk to the front door. We turned to each other and agreed that her right leg was shorter than the left.

Not only were we officially encouraged, we had some experience with short legs resulting from hip replacement surgery.

We visited in my office for several minutes. I was waiting for the sense of God's presence to manifest before we began praying. We learned a lot about Diane during the conversation. However, the sense of God's presence was missing.

In a few minutes, Lynda excused herself to visit the ladies' room. While away from us Lynda was asking God what was going on. Why was the lunch so strained with her good friend? What was going on in the office that was creating some sense of discomfort for her?

When Lynda returned, I explained that I felt a "bad spirit" was present with us in the office. I then commanded that spirit to leave. I didn't raise my voice but rather spoke normally in commanding the spirit to leave and asking God to keep it out.

Immediately each of us could feel the healing anointing of God enter the office. It felt as if the Holy Spirit came through the closed door and filled up the office. No one mentioned it at the time but when we compared notes later, it was very exciting to realize that we all had sensed God's presence beginning at the same time.

We prayed that God would grow out that right leg. We were thrilled and in awe, but no longer surprised, when the length of both legs evened out.

When it came time to leave, Diane reached for her cane. Lynda said, "Just give that cane to me."

Diane said, "I've forgotten how to walk without it."

Lynda said, "Just step out in faith and keep on walking."

Diane did exactly as instructed and cried all the way home, in awe of what God had done for her.

In our Sunday night group we had quite a mix of people. Many denominations were represented. Perhaps the only common ground was that we were all excited or at least wanted to become excited.

Art and Ginny joined us after a few weeks. Each time they came it was obvious that Art was very skeptical and Ginny was angry. They were newcomers to the church but knew a few people in the group. In the fellowship portion of our gatherings Art explained that he simply did not believe in healing. He was sure it was all a fake, starting with the televangelists he had seen on TV. Ginny owned up to being angry but didn't tell us why.

Art and Ginny showed up each Sunday night. Art was still very skeptical and Ginny was still angry, but they came each week. Nancy and I didn't understand the draw for them but we were so excited by what God was doing in our midst we welcomed anyone who might become excited with us.

Nancy and I enjoyed seeing them at church and at our house on Sunday nights. We were disappointed in Art's skepticism as we reported the miracles we were seeing but wanted desperately for that whole group to catch the wind of the Holy Spirit.

One Sunday morning, a young girl named Chelsea came to our church for the first time. She was about fifteen and was walking with crutches.

I said to her, "You can give me your crutches. You won't need them after today."

Her mother nearly jumped out of her chair. "She cannot put any weight on that left leg. She needs the crutches."

I told Chelsea, "If you aren't healed by the end of the service, come up front and we will be glad to pray for you."

That Sunday, Art and Ginny brought Beverly, a massage therapist friend, to church with them. At the end of the service several members of our Sunday night group gathered in the front of the sanctuary with Chelsea. Art inched closer to this group at the front while Ginny and Beverly visited in the middle of the sanctuary.

Chelsea explained that she had injured her left calf and was expecting to have surgery shortly because she could not put weight on left leg. We anointed her leg liberally with oil while explaining that this was not magic oil but rather a symbol of the Holy Spirit. We prayed for her just a short time and asked her to check it out.

Chelsea stood up, took about five steps away from the group, turned around and said, "Now that's just weird."

I asked, "What's weird?"

She said, "It doesn't hurt anymore."

I explained, "That's not weird. Jesus just healed you."

I started out of the sanctuary to take Chelsea's crutches to her mother who was now at the front door. I passed by Art who was dissolved in tears. I looked at him with a questioning look on my face.

Art said, "I think I just saw a legitimate miracle. That little girl's leg just got healed."

I then took her crutches to her mother while she was wiping some of the excess oil from her leg and putting her shoe back on. When I returned, Nancy was searching for me. "What's up," I asked.

Nancy explained, "Chelsea asked whether next week we could pray for her other leg because she had already had surgery on that knee but was having problems with a bone which moved around in her knee."

Naturally, we did not wait for next week. Art didn't hang back this time. He was in the middle of the group praying for Chelsea.

While we were praying for her right knee, I could feel a bone in her knee "banging" against my thumb. I looked at Chelsea's leg. She wasn't moving it. I asked her, "Are you doing that?"

She replied, "No."

"Can you feel it moving?"

"Yes."

When we finished our short prayer, we asked her to check it out. She walked around the front of the sanctuary with no pain, no limp and no problem with her knee. We thanked her for giving us the privilege of praying for her and said good-by. She walked out of the sanctuary, pain free, no limp, and no problem with her knee, while the rest of us looked at her and one another in total awe of the goodness of God.

That night, Art and Ginny brought Beverly to our house for the usual Sunday night get together. When nearly everyone else had gone home, Ginny said, "We ought to pray for Beverly."

"What's the matter with Beverly?"

"She is nearly totally deaf. She wears hearing aids in both ears and relies almost exclusively on lip reading."

I had not noticed the hearing aids because her hair covered her ears. We sat her at the dining room table and asked her to put the hearing aids on the table. The prayer for her ears was typically short and we waited for a response from Beverly. She just sat at the table with her palms open, eyes closed and not moving.

We knew that God was not done with her. We could each sense the presence of God in the room and were willing to wait and see what He was up to.

In a few minutes, Art approached Beverly and placed both of his hands on her ears and leaning close to her face prayed for her. Remember, this is the same Art who for many, many months had been skeptical about any healing but who had seen Chelsea healed that morning.

Again, Beverly just sat at the table. I was sitting behind her while Nancy, Ginny and Art were in front of her. We were talking about Beverly when I said something behind Beverly.

She said, "I heard that."

Our collective jaws dropped. Ginny was very excited. "She can't hear behind her because she can't read your lips."

Beverly said, "I can hear that."

I said, "Now, Beverly, the question is whether you put your hearing aids back in your ears to go home."

She said, "I think I will just leave them out."

By the time everyone left it was quite dark. Beverly walked ahead of Art and Ginny on the way to their cars. All the way to the cars, Art and Beverly were carrying on a conversation which Beverly could hear just fine without turning her head to see Art's lips.

Seeing Chelsea's legs healed in the morning turned Art into a person who is willing to pray for healing at the drop of a hat. He had felt for many years that God just didn't talk to him. Now he knows better. Witnessing Chelsea's miracle moved Art one giant step away from wanting to believe in God toward knowing God. He is simply not the same person now as before Chelsea's miracle.

By this time in our journey we were praying for people in restaurants, at my office, in our home, at church, and wherever folks could be found. Our confidence level continued to increase as we continued to be encouraged and moved farther from trying to believe in God to knowing Him.

Sometimes the presence of God would manifest so strongly that I would know we were supposed to pray for someone in the most unlikely circumstances. Carol is a good example.

I was meeting Nancy and our pastor at Cotton Patch for lunch. We were all coming in separate cars. I arrived first. As I was getting out of the car, a woman was getting out of the passenger side of a van parked close by. As she got out it was obvious she was quite impaired in her movements of her legs. When she produced the cane from the van I knew she was a legal target.

I asked her about her mobility problems and the cane. She explained that she had been treated for a particular cancer. Following the treatment she had been diagnosed with a disease which wastes away muscle tissue.

I explained that Nancy and our pastor were on the way and, when they arrived, we would be glad to pray with her if that would be alright.

She looked at me, seeming to take the measure of me, and decided that would be OK.

The presence of God was so strong in the parking lot I told her we would pray again once the others arrived but I felt we should pray right then. I explained about my sense of the presence of God and said, "We have learned that God's presence is His power. He doesn't leave home without it. I believe we need to pray right here in the parking lot."

After a short prayer, Carol went into the restaurant with her sister. When Nancy and our pastor arrived and we were seated I pointed out Carol and explained the parking lot encounter.

The three of us went to her booth and sat down. We visited about her condition for about three minutes, offered our best, short prayer and returned to our table. We learned that she was a personal trainer and very athletic and active prior to this current condition. She had gained considerable weight while she was immobile.

After the meal, Carol walked to our booth to thank us for praying. As she walked toward the front door it seemed to each of us that she was walking better than when she walked to our booth.

Carol and Nancy had exchanged telephone numbers. She was not from Granbury where we live. They expected to talk again.

The next morning we were driving from Granbury to Austin. While we stopped in Lampasas on the way, the phone rang. Nancy visited with Carol for a few minutes. All I could hear was excitement at Nancy's end while Carol related her story.

Carol had gotten up early that morning, put on her jogging suit and tennis shoes and gone for a walk, without her cane. She reported that she walked for a mile and felt so good that she had run for a mile. She was overcome with the enormity of what God had done for her. Nancy and I were in tears. How in the world had we been fortunate enough to get into the center of this wonder and amazement?

For each person who we saw God heal, we knew that God had changed their history. It was really fun to see someone who was healed on Wednesday still healed the next week, the next month and on and on. These significant changes in history were truly awe-inspiring.

The best part for Nancy and me was more than seeing God change our history and the history of those we were seeing healed. God had become solidly real for us. He was no longer a theory we longed to believe, hoped was true and relied upon for eternal life. Now we knew without a shadow of a doubt that He is real, that we could take Jesus at His word, and that He was intimately concerned with all the details of our lives. We had *believed* that God was good all the time. Now we *knew* it.

Now we understood better what James was addressing when he wrote,

> *If any of you lacks wisdom, he should ask God, who gives generously to all without finding fault, and it will be given to him. But when he asks, he must believe and not doubt, because he who doubts is like*

> *a wave of the sea, blown and tossed by the wind.*
> *That man should not think he will receive anything*
> *from the Lord; he is a double-minded man, unstable*
> *in all he does.* (James 1:5-8)

Jesus also encouraged his disciples to believe even before you receive.

> *"I tell you the truth, if anyone says to this mountain,*
> *'Go, throw yourself into the sea,' and does not doubt*
> *in his heart but believes that what he says will*
> *happen, it will be done for him. Therefore I tell you,*
> *whatever you ask for in prayer, believe that you have*
> *received it, and it will be yours."* (Mark 11:23-24)

A large part of the renewing of your mind is elimination of double-mindedness. God provides evidence of His presence, His power and His love when He heals His people. Each healing becomes part of the testimony of Jesus. The revelation knowledge that comes from witnessing miracle after miracle chases double-mindedness away.

CHAPTER NINE
Doing What Jesus Did

*I tell you the truth, anyone who has faith in me will
do what I have been doing. He will do even greater
things than these, because I am going to the Father.
And I will do whatever you ask in my name, so that
the Son may bring glory to the Father. You may ask
me for anything in my name, and I will do it. (John
14:12-14)*

Jesus promised I will do those things He had been doing. The
only prerequisite is faith in Jesus. All believers are included.

Jesus did not say I *can do* what He had been doing but
rather that I *will do* those things. Have you noticed that everything
the Bible tells us to do is *impossible*? Apart from Jesus I can do
nothing. (John 15:5)

If I *will do* certain things, I must be authorized to access the
power necessary to perform the tasks. Jesus did not say that I *will*
participate in things in the kingdom only to withhold access to
the power to get those things done.

Jesus could only do what He saw the Father doing. (John 5:19)
If I am going to do the things Jesus did, I will need to know what

121

the Father is doing. Miraculous healing will never be my province. It shall remain the province of the Father who determines who, when and how.

In order to heal the sick, Jesus had to ascertain whether the power of the Lord was present and what the Father was healing at that time. He also needed to know whether the power to heal was to be applied to all who were there or only to a select few. Thinking about these issues furnishes valuable insight into Jesus' prayers.

We know that *"Jesus often withdrew to lonely places and prayed."* (Luke 5:16) What do you suppose He was praying about? He did not spend one split second on confessing his sins—He had none. He likely did not pray for his daily bread. After all, He knew how to take what was available, give thanks for it, and then watch as the Father increased the supply to fill the need. Isn't that exactly what He did at the wedding feast in Cana? (John 2:1-10) Isn't that exactly what He did at the feeding of the five thousand and the four thousand? (Matthew 14:15-21; Matthew 15:32-28)

Jesus must have prayed to learn *where* the Father was acting, *upon whom* the Father would be pouring out His compassion, and *what* was the nature of the problem. Scripture records only one person being healed beside the pool at Bethesda. There may have been others healed that day. Or, there may not! Jesus needed to know which man had God's attention that day. Jesus likewise needed to know whether the Father was only healing that day or was He also teaching, preaching or delivering from torment.

Consider the raising of Lazarus. (John 11:1-44) There was a delay of three or four days from the time that Jesus knew of Lazarus' condition until he was raised from the dead. Jesus loved Lazarus. He surely wanted, in his humanity, to get to Lazarus as soon as possible to see him raised. Yet, the Father apparently had a significant delay in mind. Only when the Father was prepared to raise Lazarus from the dead was the Spirit of the Lord present for raising Lazarus. Jesus knew from the beginning that the end result would not be death. Rather, the Father was acting in the circumstances for His glory so that Jesus could be glorified through raising Lazarus to life. (John 11:4) Until the Father was raising Lazarus, Jesus had no power to do so.

What Do We Do?

There is no magic formula for healing. You need not learn any formula because you won't be doing it. All healing is done by God. We are merely by-standers and co-laborers.

Nancy and I try to discern what the Father is doing before we begin praying for anyone. Our inquiry is made on several fronts.

Ask the person. Let the person seeking healing explain what is desired or what the problem is. Do not cut this step short. We have often seen people launch into prayers for someone either without asking what the problem is or with an incomplete understanding of the nature of the problem. Those same people seem to be in a hurry to "get out of Dodge" when they are done with their prayers.

If the person is not sure how to start, you can say, "tell me where it hurts." Many times, the person requesting prayer will offer insights into the nature and source of the problem. Gentle, probing questions often illuminate a fuller picture of what is needed.

Don't be in a hurry to start praying. The person's answers do not necessarily tell us what the Father is doing but rather the person's understanding of the need. The answers seldom tell us *all* the Father is doing.

I will usually follow-up with "What else?" Our experience has taught us that the full picture seldom comes out in this first part of the interview. Many times the person requesting prayer views some matters as either too big or too insignificant for God. We attempt to get it all on the table.

Remember, Jesus asked Bartimaeus "What do you want me to do for you?" (Mark 10:51) In essence Jesus gave Bartimaeus a blank check. He asked for his sight. His sight is all he got. What if he had asked for more? We like to ask God to empty the entire heavenly warehouse of blessing with that person's name on it by delivering every blessing that very day. We want to leave nothing behind simply because we did not ask.

Listen to the person. Listen to the answer of where it hurts and give plenty of time to receive other complaints. You will often find the root cause of several problems when you get the whole picture. Does this person have any insight into when, why and how any of these afflictions began?

I find that when people give you the whole picture they are sometimes overwhelmed with the enormity of the storm in their life. They speak as if they own each problem, disease or condition. My response to these people is to remind them of the size of God rather than the size of the storm. I will usually say, "Boy, I was afraid you might have something serious."

Listen to the Holy Spirit. While listening to the answer from the person, we have learned to also listen to the Holy Spirit. An unspoken question to the Holy Spirit about what is going on often provides insights into the source or true nature of the problem. A surprising number of physical ailments coincide with some spiritual difficulty or some hurtful experience. We believe that praying for the sick, injured or tormented is simply not complete without inquiring of the Holy Spirit what else is going on.

The Holy Spirit provides words of knowledge about conditions that the person may not have in focus. When you get that sense, inquire about specific problems. Don't be afraid to ask whether there is pain in a particular part of the body if the Holy Spirit has suggested to you there is.

Continue listening while praying. While the prayer continues, keep seeking the mind of the Holy Spirit about what else is happening. It is not uncommon to start praying for one issue and end up praying for another apparently unrelated issue.

Once the dam breaks all the water can come out. When the Holy Spirit and the person are apparently done describing the nature and source of the problem, we assume that we have heard all we will hear and have seen all we will see as to what the Father is doing—until we start praying.

During the prayer, we watch the person. I don't believe God closes His eyes when we pray. We are perfectly capable of praying with our eyes open. We pay attention to such things as heat in the body, trembling and other uncommon phenomena. We don't hesitate to point out to the person that a part or all of his body is becoming very hot. We explain that the physical phenomenon is a manifestation of God's presence and power.

If Nancy notices gold dust or gold sparkles on her hands while we are praying, we point this out. We once again explain this is another manifestation of God's presence and power. Often when we point out the gold dust, we find that the person being prayed for has gold dust on them also. This manifestation is a real encourager for the person receiving prayer, not to mention to us.

I often feel electric with a whole body goose bump while praying for people. It seems the closer the prayer comes to the real issue that God is healing, the more likely it is that I will feel the electricity. When I feel electric I explain that I am sensing the presence of God in a manner I often sense his presence while people have been healed. I am careful to explain that God doesn't heal because I feel electric but rather I feel electric when God is healing.

Don't hurry. Our prayers tend to be of short duration. We don't believe that God needs a consultant or an advisor on what to do to heal the person. We are partial to the eight words Moses used in praying for Miriam to be healed of leprosy. "*Heal her now, Oh God, I beseech thee.*" (Numbers 12:13)

Miraculous healing often continues well after the active prayer is concluded. We often get done before God does. Through time we have been able to sense that God is still acting. In those circumstances, we do not hesitate to tell the person being prayed for to wait expectantly because God is not done yet. Don't feel you need to keep babbling prayers just because God is still working. Just wait. You may be led to pray further at a later stage of the process.

Check for results. When you perceive that God is done acting, ask the person to "check it out." Ask them to do something he couldn't do before without pain. If he couldn't move his ankle, ask him to move his ankle. If the condition is improved but not perfect, do not hesitate to pray again. Do not be afraid to repeat or continue your prayers if you encounter a "trees walking" experience.

We will often request the person receiving prayer to take some action. "Walk to the exit sign and return here." The nature of the action seems to be incidental. What we have observed is that the healing many times manifests as the person is taking action. How would the man beside the pool at Bethesda know he had been healed if he had not gotten up, taken his mat and gone home?

Beware of "canned" prayers. If you know in advance the words you will use, be cautious. Many who have prayed fervently for years for issues such as back pain may develop a formula "back prayer" irrespective of whether or not that prayer has been effective in the past. The person requesting prayer will receive the formula "back prayer" and assume that is the end of the issue.

When others start the prayer immediately it seems to interfere with my ability to hear from God about the nature and extent of the problem. I sometimes simply wait until the "formula prayers" are concluded and then start a gentle inquiry. Occasionally, a word of knowledge or wisdom will come during the "formula prayers" but the formula prayers are so distracting that I find it more difficult to hear.

Remember that Jesus the man did not become *able* to heal following His Baptism with the Holy Spirit. Neither did we. We still are completely dependent upon God's power for healing, whether instantly or over time. It simply isn't us. Since Jesus couldn't do it, I am confident I cannot do it. Miraculous healing starts and ends with God. This knowledge reinforces the need to see and hear what the Father is doing.

Be prepared for falling. There is no discernable healing benefit from allowing someone to fall on the floor. If you do not have "catchers," have the person you are praying for sit down. It is easier to hold them in the chair than to try to ease them to the floor.

What about Qualifications?

I can't do what God alone can do. However, I can do what a man in right relation to God the Father did, and greater things than these. All I need is access to the same power and authorization to use it.

To access the same power that Jesus relied on, I need to have the same standing before the Father as Jesus had. The good news is that we have that very same standing. Because of what Jesus did, we are the righteousness of God in Christ.

> *Therefore, if anyone is in Christ, he is a new creation; the old has gone, the new has come! . . . God made*

> *him who had no sin to be sin for us, so that in*
> *him we might become the righteousness of God.* (2
> Corinthians 5:17-21)

We stand before God the Father in the same earthly shoes that Jesus wore. Jesus was in good standing before God because He committed no sin. God is no longer counting our sins against us. Jesus is the righteousness of God. We become the righteousness of God through faith in Jesus.

What is the source of this righteousness? Faith in Jesus. What is the source of our salvation? Faith in Jesus. What is the only prerequisite to do those things Jesus had been doing? Faith in Jesus. Do I detect a pattern here?

No Rules

When Nancy and I taught our first class on miracles, signs and wonders, the participants came from many different denominational backgrounds. In one of the first sessions, we asked about the "rules" for healing which the class members had been taught through the years. In short order, we had a list of twenty-five "rules" which people genuinely believed concerning miracles, signs and wonders. Most of those rules attempted to tie actions and attitudes, either on the part of the person praying or on the part of the person requesting prayer, to God's willingness to miraculously heal.

None of the rules we discussed are true. Each formula offered has been completely debunked by our experience. In each instance, the prior reported miraculous healing violated one or more of the rules (and quite often all of them). It has become apparent the "rules" for healing are not rules after all. The "rules" were born out of an attempt to explain the apparent lack of manifestation of a miraculous healing. The "rules" clearly have no causative effect. Rather, they were excuses for no results.

We know without a doubt that we can do nothing by ourselves. Jesus is the healer, every time, not us. God heals His people not because they are good, not because the people praying for them are good, but because He is good.

Jesus never refused to perform a miraculous healing. It is not in the book. Peter explained to the centurion, Cornelius, and his household:

> "*God anointed Jesus of Nazareth with the Holy Ghost and with power: who went about doing good, and healing all that were oppressed of the devil; for God was with him.*" (Acts 10:38 KJV)

Jesus did not heal *some* that were oppressed of the devil. He healed *all* who were oppressed of the devil. Scripture recounts many instances in which Jesus healed them *all*. (Matthew 4:24; 8:16; 9:35; 12:15; 14:36; Mark 6:56; Luke 4:40; 6:19)

Theology Is Based On What God Is Doing

The renewed mind can accept the promises Jesus made. No matter how many promises God has made, Jesus is the divine yes to them all. (2 Corinthians 1:20) We have decided to take Jesus at His word.

The testimony of Jesus is what Jesus did and said. The testimony of Jesus does not include what *apparently* did *not* happen. Guesses and surmises of what was *not perceived* serve no purpose. There is no prophecy involved there. The atmosphere will not be changed by a recitation of what was not observed. The creative power of the Word of God is not involved with reports of what apparently did not happen.

The scriptures are clear that Jesus healed all who were afflicted by the devil. That is the standard. That is the truth. Do not accept any lesser standard.

Theology Is Not Based On What God Did Not Do

Be particularly cautious when "interpreting" God's word to discern rules or biblical principles concerning miraculous healing. It is dangerous to think that we can turn over a coin and properly interpret the other side. It is much safer to take Jesus at His word rather than try to figure out what Jesus would have announced in a different circumstance. In this context, it is dangerous to construct a theology to attempt to explain why a healing was not manifested in a particular instance. We have no scripture precedent for such rules.

We do not have the ability to completely comprehend what Jesus is doing and when He is doing it. An *apparent* lack of a miraculous healing tells us nothing.

Just Because We Didn't See It Doesn't Mean It Didn't Happen

Our powers of observation are extremely limited. We have no power to observe the seed of healing planted at the time of our prayer. The seed may grow for a period of time before the healing is manifested to our senses. We believe it is impossible to pray consistent with the will of God and have nothing happen. If we don't see it happen, that means nothing about whether a seed was deposited or not.

An example of the limitations of our powers of observation is the wedding feast in Cana. When Jesus turned the water into wine, no one knew *when* the miracle occurred. There was a manifestation at the pouring of the wine that the water had been transformed. But, who knew? The master of the banquet did not know that the wine had ever been bath water.

Scripture does not disclose who knew of the miracle, when it occurred, or even whether one had been attempted! No one had the complete picture but God Himself.

The occurrence of the miracle did not necessarily coincide with the perception of the miracle. Indeed, there was no perception there had been a miracle until the master had complimented the bridegroom on the best wine. (John 2:1-10)

CHAPTER TEN

What about Claude?

God anointed Jesus of Nazareth with the Holy Spirit and with power and he went around doing good and healing all who were under the power of the devil, because God was with him. (Acts 10:38)

Authentic experience with miracles, signs and wonders is rare. As a consequence, many explanations have been offered through the years why the promises found in the Bible are not manifested in your life today. Those explanations constitute a theology based upon **lack of observation** of the truth and reliability of Jesus' promise:

I tell you the truth, anyone who has faith in me will do what I have been doing. He will do even greater things than these, because I am going to the Father. And I will do whatever you ask in my name, so that the Son may bring glory to the Father. You may ask me for anything in my name, and I will do it. (John 14:12-14)

The church has always known better than to claim that Jesus was either deluded or a liar. So, various rules and explanations have apparently evolved through years of lack to explain why:

o "anyone" doesn't mean "anyone" in all circumstances; those aren't the things Jesus was doing;
o Jesus is not doing those things anymore;
o the promise was given only to validate the ministry of a select few;
o there really are quantitative criteria for faith in Jesus which must be met first;
o there are restrictions on "whatever you ask;
o there are restrictions on asking "in my name"; and
o the promise was restricted to a select few gifted people.

Three Theological Camps

Cessationists.

There are those who believe that miracles, signs and wonders are not for today. This belief has long been held by many religious intellectuals and is based upon identifiable scriptures. One explanation of this theology of lack is found in the notorious 1934 debate between Elder Ben M. Bogard and Aimee Semple McPherson. Dr. Bogard was the Pastor of the Antioch Missionary Baptist Church, Little Rock, Arkansas. Aimee Semple McPherson was the founder of the Four Square Gospel Church, which had its headquarters at Angelus Temple, Los Angeles, California. Dr. Bogard was a cessationist. Mrs. McPherson was on the other side of the issue. The debate was stenographically reported by J.

E. Rhodes and is available on many internet sites today. (See for example, *www.padfield.com*)

The proposition for the debate was:

"Divine healing and miracles as taught and manifest in the Word of God ceased with the Apostolic Age."

Dr. Bogard argued that God used miracles, signs and wonders solely to validate a messenger. If signs and wonders followed a preacher, he could be trusted. Dr. Bogard believed the canonization of the New Testament furnished the means for validation of a preacher. He felt it was no longer necessary for God to confirm a preacher's ministry by miraculous demonstrations of His power.

Apparently, Dr. Bogard did not understand that God heals His children physically, mentally and emotionally because He loves them.

Dr. Bogard was so convinced that the works of the Holy Spirit had passed away that he refused to believe that anyone had ever been healed through Aimee Semple McPherson's ministry. Indeed, he said if he saw someone healed on the stage before him he would know that the devil did it, not God.

Jesus, Himself, had told the Pharisees to not believe His words but rather to believe the miracles. (John 10:25; John 10:37-38; John 14:11) Even Jesus was accused of casting out demons by the power of Beelzebub. (Matthew 12:24)

For those in this cessationist camp, revelation knowledge is required for renewing the mind to permit these folks to participate in delivering God's compassion to His people. Even witnessing miraculous physical, emotional and mental healings are viewed with intense suspicion. Was the person really afflicted? Who performed the healing, God or the devil? Only revelation knowledge can break through that dam.

Those Needing An Experience.

A second camp is those people who believe intellectually in miracles, signs and wonders but don't experience them. This chapter is aimed primarily at those in this camp.

Those with an intellectual belief in miracles, signs and wonders but no experience are imprisoned by a culture of highly developed unbelief. The limitations which trap things in our minds usually take root from scripture taken out of context or misquoted. Scripture misquoted over a long period of time does not make it true. It is still a lie.

Each time you pray for someone and do not discern the immediate manifestation of the result you asked for, you are at risk of trapping miracles, signs and wonders in your mind. It is easy to either embrace one of the erroneous rules why God's promise was not true *this time*, or to decide that God's promise is only true for *other people*.

Escaping these traps requires a renewed mind. God does not lower the scriptural bar to embrace our lack of perception. We are not excused from healing the sick because we didn't see what we wanted on occasion.

Wait, you say, we can't heal the sick. I know! When Jesus sent out the twelve, he gave them an impossible task.

> As you go, preach this message: 'The kingdom of heaven is near.' Heal the sick, raise the dead, cleanse those who have leprosy, drive out demons. Freely you have received, freely give. (Matthew 10:7-8)

The fact that the twelve could not, of themselves, heal the sick did not change the job. Their job was to heal the sick.

Jesus did not give us a job and then fail to equip us to complete the job.

The good news is that the journey from the second camp to this third camp is easy.

<u>Those Experiencing Miracles.</u>

The third camp is those people who believe in miracles, signs and wonders and experience them as part of the normal Christian life. Claude's story is offered to get those in the second camp "on the bus" and headed for the third camp.

Who is Claude, Anyway?

Claude and his wife Connie are friends we met in Ruidoso. In his pre-Ruidoso life Claude had been a pastor of a Baptist church in Texas. There is a wide range of belief and teaching about the Holy Spirit in today's Baptist Church. Claude did not deny that the Holy Spirit was working today but he had not focused on spiritual gifts in his ministry at the time we started meeting with him.

Connie was more drawn to spiritual gifts than was Claude. Connie's hunger for more kept her returning to questions about spiritual gifts.

Claude and Connie are both trained as insurance claims adjusters for catastrophic storms. They traveled together before we met them. After they moved to Ruidoso, Claude traveled alone more often than not.

We discussed our beliefs about baptism in the Holy Spirit with Claude just before he traveled to Texas for an adjusting trip. He listened carefully but we knew he would need to search out the scriptures himself and make up his own mind.

Upon Claude's return from Texas, he reported that he had studied the Gospels and had become impressed that baptism in the Holy Spirit was included in each one. If it is in all four

Gospels, he reasoned, it must be important. He was unwilling to "read out" references to this baptism and the spiritual gifts.

His attitude about tongues was basically, "If God wants me to have that gift He can give it to me." He asked that we pray with him for Baptism in the Holy Spirit on the night before he left for an adjusting job in Hurricane Katrina. We were happy to join with him asking for the equipping that comes with Baptism in the Holy Spirit.

By the time he returned from Katrina, Claude was dangerous. The next time he preached in the Baptist Church he explained the benefit of and the need for Baptism in the Holy Spirit. He encountered some questions! Nancy and I had moved to Granbury by that time so were didn't hear it in person. However, we certainly enjoyed the reports of the sermon and the reaction.

Adverse Diagnosis

In 2008, Connie called us from Houston and reported, "Claude and I are in Houston. I have been diagnosed with rheumatoid arthritis. We will be returning to Ruidoso soon."

I asked, "Has anyone prayed for you there."

"Oh yes," Connie reported. "Claude has been part of a good Sunday school class her in Houston and the leader has prayed for me."

I found myself saying, "Connie, this will sound egotistical but I wish you would come by Granbury on your way home to Ruidoso and give us a chance to pray for you. We have been seeing some amazing things."

I was chagrined that my statement made it sound like our group was something special. After all, someone had already prayed for her. How dare I believe that our prayers would be more effective? I didn't have any theology to support that belief. However, I believed it nonetheless.

For those who are unfamiliar with Texas geography, Granbury is not on the route from Houston to Ruidoso. I knew I was asking for a substantial side trip but felt compelled to make the offer.

We contacted several people in Granbury who had prayed with us before and had seen some amazing results. We also contacted some members of our church who we knew often received words of knowledge and wisdom. We were anxious to pray for Connie.

The First Installment

Claude and Connie arrived in Granbury in a few days. A group assembled at our house. I reported to Claude and Connie the miracles we had witnessed and the experience we had with words of knowledge about the people for whom we prayed. I was giving the testimony of Jesus.

We prayed for Connie first. There were at least two words of knowledge given about what God was doing for her, neither of which appeared to have anything to do with rheumatoid arthritis. We then prayed for her and hoped for the best. We could not imagine how she could check whether God had done anything for her RA.

Then we asked Claude if he wanted prayer about anything. He gladly accepted. We asked him what we would be praying for.

He said, "I am pretty intrigued by these words of knowledge. Let's just see what you come up with."

When we started praying, I said, "Father God I ask that you would show Claude what you are doing so that he will only do what you are doing and only say what you are saying."

Others offered prayers for issues I do not recall.

After the prayers, Claude said, "That was very interesting. There are two other areas I would like addressed. My neck is very sore and my right ankle will not extend."

He demonstrated for us the limited motion he had in his right ankle as a result of a severe automobile accident in 2001. His surgeon had recommended fusing his ankle. Claude had opted for a metal plate and several screws in his ankle. Through a short period of time his ankle had basically become fused at a ninety degree angle from his leg. He was unable to extend his right foot toward the floor.

We prayed for those two issues. When asked to check it out, Claude reported his neck pain was gone but that there was no change in his ankle.

We explained about Jesus and the man who saw men as trees walking. I said, "We are going to pray again."

Claude was sitting in a chair with both feet up on a large round ottoman/coffee table in our living room. Janice, our foot-praying specialist, had her hands on Claude's right ankle. (I say Janice was our "foot specialist" even though I have never heard her pray out loud for anything. However, when feet were healed or legs grew out, Janice had her hands on the focal point.) Janice said, "I see that metal plate turning into flexible plastic." Then we prayed.

After we were done praying, I opened my eyes to see Claude dissolved in tears. I asked him what the problem was.

He said, "I can't do that." He was pointing to his right ankle which was fully extended.

I said, "It seems like you are doing it now."

He reported, "I have not been able to do that for many years."

We were all quite excited about a metal plate that Janice had seen turning into flexible plastic. Whether that happened in the physical realm or not, the result was Claude's ankle functioned properly for the first time since 2001.

The next morning we awoke to find Claude missing. When he finally returned to our house, I asked where he had been.

He said, "I just took my new ankle for a test drive."

Claude, Connie, Nancy and I then went to a restaurant for breakfast. We were all very excited about Claude's ankle. While we discussed the prayers of the previous day, Connie reported, "I think it's cool that God is going to heal the root of my problem before He heals the RA."

Claude then asked, "Jeff, before you guys prayed for me had you been talking to Connie about what was going on with me?"

"No," I said. "We had not had time for that."

Claude said, "I was wondering how you knew to pray for the exact issues God has been dealing with me about."

I said, "I just prayed what first came to my mind. I have no idea what God is dealing with you about."

Claude said, "The ankle thing was great but I was more impressed that several of you knew exactly what to pray for without asking me."

At that time I was reading the debate between Dr. Bogard and Aimee Semple McPherson. I told Claude, "Someone needs to ask the cessationists, 'what about Claude.'" He had not only reported relief from pain in his neck but he could now move a joint that, for all practical purposes, had been fused for more than seven years.

Connie was not short-changed. She returned to Ruidoso with Claude before filling any of the prescriptions for treatment of the diagnosed RA. More than three years later she still has not taken any medication for the RA and has no symptoms.

The Second Installment

After Art and Ginny had seen Chelsea healed in the sanctuary at our church and prayed and seen Beverly receive her hearing, we planned a trip to Ruidoso. I called Connie to see whether we could stay with them while we were in Ruidoso.

Connie said, "Sure. You don't know about Claude. He was in Colorado doing insurance adjusting and was in a rear-end collision on the interstate. He has two broken vertebrae in his back, has severe pain radiating down his leg and is in pretty sorry shape."

I said, "We will be there tomorrow and we'll pray for him."

Art, Ginny, Nancy and I arrived the following day in Ruidoso to find Claude in his chair in the living room. He was wearing a back brace for his two broken vertebrae and a TENS unit to help control the pain radiating into his legs.

Claude said, "I spend pretty much of my day right here in my chair."

We visited with him about the accident which caused these injuries and the type of pain he was experiencing. After this conversation, we prayed a short prayer for Claude. When he checked it out, he reported things were vastly improved. He did not wear his back brace any longer that day and did not sleep in it that night. He no longer used the TENS unit. We were all thrilled but not surprised.

The following day, Claude took his back brace with him to physical therapy but only wore it for a few minutes. He took it off because he did not need it and has never put it back on.

The pain radiating into his legs is gone. The pain in his back is gone. He back brace spent a few days beside his chair in the living room. After a few days, Connie asked him to get that brace out of the living room.

Claude called his neurosurgeon and cancelled his appointment.

The Third Installment

In his first accident in 2001, Claude's stomach became attached to his abdominal wall because of the scar tissue caused by his feeding tube. He had experienced no stomach issues since 2001.

In the 2009 accident, Claude's stomach became dislodged from its prior connection to his abdomen. He had a hernia in his chest which permitted his stomach to "ride up" in his chest so that it was higher than it should be and too close to his lungs and heart.

On New Year's Day, 2010, Claude underwent surgery in Dallas to reposition his stomach and attach it again to his abdominal wall so that it would not "ride up" any longer. We visited him the day following the surgery. Connie was at her son's house at the time of our visit so we were in the room with Claude alone.

When we inquired how he was doing, Claude reported, "I'm on an IV drip of morphine so I don't hurt anywhere except in my left shoulder. That pain is intense and the morphine doesn't touch it."

I said, "Claude, I think that problem is coming out of your neck."

He said, "No, my neck feels fine. The problem is pain in the shoulder."

Nancy and I prayed for him. I got behind his hospital bed so that I could get my hands on his neck. Nancy was positioned beside the bed so she could put her hands on his hands or arms. The minute I put my hand on his neck, the pain in his shoulder stopped. We didn't know that so we offered a short prayer. However, the shoulder pain had already stopped before we began praying.

143

The Fourth Installment

Over the next two years, Claude continued to be pain free in his back, legs and ankle. He took several out of state assignments for insurance adjusting following catastrophic storms.

Connie and Claude both noticed significant changes in Claude's ability to organize his work processes, memory changes, and other issues which caused some alarm. They sought help from health care professionals who diagnosed a long-term brain injury. Medication helped somewhat. Claude had suffered a significant concussion in high school, the 2001 accident and then the 2009 accident. These incidents combined were causing his current problems.

Claude experienced no lack of intelligence. He still was a gifted preacher, often filling in at his church in Ruidoso. His problems manifested primarily in long-term assignments in the insurance adjusting arena. The individual tasks all went well. However, the final result was sometimes out of reach.

Nancy and I shared a report over the phone with Connie of a child who we believed had been healed at our church in part by God healing his incompletely formed brain stem. Connie felt strongly that Claude would benefit from prayer at the healing room of our church. Our healing room is staffed for an hour prior to the service each Sunday.

Claude was returning from an insurance adjusting assignment in the eastern United States and met up with Connie in the Dallas area. We were pleased to meet them for dinner in Arlington. At that dinner we reported to Claude about the child's healing and the remarkable changes we had seen in him. We invited Claude to come to the healing room on Sunday before church so the team there could pray for him.

Claude arrived in the healing room that Sunday. The team in the healing room visited with Claude for several minutes to try to "understand" the nature of the brain injury and how it would manifest. Before we prayed for Claude, we had a short prayer asking the Father what He would be doing for Claude that morning so that we could be co-laborers with Him.

Four of the five people who were going to pray for Claude all received the same word of knowledge about Claude's condition. That word was shared with Claude and then we began to pray.

It is common for the people receiving prayer to become very hot prior to and during the prayer. We have experienced times when the entire room seems to become overheated. As we all prayed for Claude he became so hot that he was sweating. His t-shirt was quite wet by the end of the prayer. Each of us praying for him became quite hot.

Claude stayed for our Sunday service and sat with us. He seemed to have a new-found peace about him. He was not yet ready to share with us what changes he had experienced.

The following Saturday night we joined Claude and Connie for dinner. He seemed to be different person. He was peaceful in a way we had not seen for several years.

Connie said, "Let me just say "thank you, Jesus' for giving me my husband back." Pointing at Claude she said, "This is the guy I married. I'm glad to have him back."

About one month later I spoke with Claude by telephone. I had heard good reports from others about seeing a difference in Claude. Now I could get a report "from the horse's mouth."

Claude reported that he was doing much better in the affected areas. He felt he no longer needed his medications so he had discontinued them. Even without the medication, he was doing well. He was scheduled to see his doctor the following morning to discuss Claude's decision to stop the medications.

After I hung up the phone, Nancy and I looked at each other and said, "He has done it again!"

Important Lessons

There are several important lessons to take away from these reports of Claude's multiple healings.

- o God's healing is not a "one-and-done" proposition. We have seen God heal the same person of several different problems at different times. You need not worry about "going to the well" too often.
- o The power of the Holy Spirit is still healing people miraculously today, even if those people started out unsure whether spiritual gifts are for today.
- o You can expect to see immediate results to your prayers for healing in many instances. You should not expect only gradual improvement over a long period of time.
- o The fullness of God's healing does not coincide with your prayers. God often does not wait for us to start praying before beginning the healing process. He also doesn't stop the healing process when we are done praying. He starts when He wants and takes the time He wants. The fullness of His healing is not limited to what we observe during the prayer.
- o All the healing was done by God and God alone. All of the prayers were addressed exclusively to God the Father, Son and Holy Spirit.
- o None of this healing was a product of anything done by the liar. The liar causes pain and discomfort. Jesus paid the price for Claude's many healings. The liar does not benefit from that payment.

CHAPTER ELEVEN
All Miracles Are Equal

Everyone who witnesses God's power in delivering His compassion to His people would like to see the flashy stuff. We want the blind to see, the lame to walk and the dead to be raised, while we are asking for it. While it is OK to desire to see the flashy stuff, it is important to recognize that we are unable under our own power to heal a blister, have a headache diminish in its pain, or bring relief to the mind and emotions of our fellow man. If those "minor" things occur while you are praying for someone, rejoice. Only God can do that! If He is on the job, you are assured of success. Celebrate His greatness, His majesty, His authority and His power without denigrating the experience by thinking, "Oh, it was only a headache."

Our experience has been quite exciting from the first miracle to the most recent. Each one has left us shaking our heads, saying, "Honey, He did it again!" Being in His presence when He delivers His compassion to His people is simply exhilarating. Yet, the liar will want to suggest that "small" miracles do not involve the power of God. You will be bombarded with thoughts like:

- o It was just time for that condition to clear up.
- o She wasn't really sick anyway.
- o This is just the power of positive thinking.
- o She's reporting an improvement just to get us off her back.
- o You think God wasted His time dealing with *that?*

Don't take the bait. If God Himself intervened in the history of that person and you were given the privilege of participating with Him, celebrate irrespective of the importance the world would give to the outcome.

We have seen a series of interventions by God concerning what seem to be increasingly more serious problems. In the parable of the minas, the King rewards his servants who stewarded his minas to earn more minas. The reward for the servant is not more minas but greater authority. (Luke 19:13-26)

God looks for people who can be trustworthy in a small matter before He gives them greater authority. Demonstrating this trustworthiness is one of the steps in the renewing of your mind. As we rely on God more and more fully and for more "significant" matters, it seems He increases our opportunities. We can almost hear God saying, "You ain't seen nothing yet."

We have already related many of the healings we have witnessed in the context of the testimony of Jesus and the progression of shoulder healings and the confidence builders we witnessed in the early days. Some of the shoulder testimonies are quite remarkable but the least of them still involved God's benevolent intervention in a life of His child to change history.

For several years it seemed we were reporting healings which occurred in the community to our church friends, hoping they would get excited. The response for awhile was basically, "How nice for you." We were not being successful in helping our church friends become confident enough to enter the arena. They would bring people to us. They would bring people to our house on Sunday nights. But, they lacked the courage to pray without outside support.

Nancy and I didn't fully apprehend the situation because we were involved with praying for people in all manner of places for all manner of problems. We saw fantastic results everywhere but in the church building itself. We even saw amazing things happen there but the opportunities presented themselves less regularly.

As You Go

We often have the opportunity to pray for someone in a "non-traditional" place. People look at us with this funny, quizzical look when we report what has become "normal" for us. We have witnessed God healed people in the following circumstances:

o an optometrist in her office during an appointment for her to examine my eyes. She went next door to the glasses store to see if they could do the prescription she wanted to give me. She left the office sick and returned well.

o a dental hygienist in her office after she finished cleaning my teeth.

o an assistant to two sculptors who were doing quick miniature busts at the civic center while we were "sitting" for them and the pubic was passing by.

o a framing contractor sitting in my office after discussing his litigation.

o a woman from Kenya who sat next to me at conference waiting for Todd Bentley to speak.

o several people walking with canes or limps we ran into in fast food restaurants.

o   the guitarist performing at a concert starring him and one other person.

We have seen God heal His people in traditional places, like church. We have seen God heal:

o   a man who needed relief from pain over his entire right side of his body. His pain on his right side was completely removed and the pain in both knees was removed.

o   the man who had pain in both knees removed a few weeks later witnessed his wife receive a complete relief of pain in her left knee.

o   a woman who had severe back pain as a result of scoliosis. The pain was relieved and an x-ray about one week later showed no scoliosis.

o   a man who walked with a four footed cane as a result of crushed vertebrae in his low back had his pain removed and no longer needed the cane.

o   a painting contractor who had injured his knee (hyperextension) had his pain removed.

o   several people using a cane had pain removed in their legs and strength restored so the cane was no longer necessary.

In each of these instances, we have stood in awe of God's power and how reliably He is pouring out His compassion on His people.

Took Our Breath Away

God has expanded our authority. God has healed some people of conditions and in circumstances which we can scarcely comprehend. At this writing, these are the instances that have made the greatest impact on us. We have felt, in each instance, this was a new high-water mark. Even though we feel completely blown away, we are confident that God has greater things in store. He is, after all, the God who is able to do exceedingly, abundantly above all that we can ask or imagine. (Ephesians 3:20)

A Breakthrough In Little Things.

Over the years, Nancy and I have prayed for many people suffering from colds and sinus related issues. Neither of us can recall significant results of those prayers.

Nancy and I try to have a "movie date" on Friday afternoons if at all possible. We will drive in to Fort Worth (the "big city" for us). Drucilla works at a movie theater we like to attend. She has been there since it opened but we had never talked to her other than to say "two, please."

One Friday, we mistakenly arrived an hour ahead of our movie time. There was no one in line to buy tickets. I looked at Drucilla and could easily see she was in distress. I said, "You're having a hard time. What's up?"

She replied, "I have had a sinus infection for more than a week. My head is killing me. I have a lot of mucus in my head and throat. I have a cough and I can't sleep well."

I asked, "Are you ready to get rid of all that?"

"Sure," she said, not really expecting anything to happen other than we would pay for our tickets.

"Can you move to the end of the counter where Nancy and I could get our hands on you to pray for you?"

"No, my boss is watching me and I have to stay right here."

I asked her to give us her hands over the counter. Nancy had one and I had one. We prayed with her very quickly to avoid causing her any problems. I then said, "Check it out. How are you?"

She breathed through her nose quite freely and said, "It seems to be clearing up."

Nancy and I then went into the snack bar to eat something prior to the movie. We had time to kill. Drucilla walked through the snack bar in about one-half hour. I asked, "How are you?" She reported that her head felt much better and her breathing was clear.

We went back to the same movie theater the following Tuesday. Drucilla was once again behind the counter. "Well, tell me about it," I said.

She reported, "The mucus changed from green to clear pretty quickly. My headaches went away. I was able to sleep. All coughing stopped. What do you make of that?"

I said, "You know exactly what happened. Jesus healed you right on the spot."

She said, "I know you are right."

This incident took our breath away because God had now healed someone in an area where we previously had no success. We were anxious to see what lay ahead.

A few weeks later, I had a cracked wisdom tooth extracted by a maxillofacial surgeon. I opted for general anesthetic because I am a baby about pain and didn't want to know anything about what was happening to me. I hate pain and I hate having my teeth cleaned or worked on in any way.

Eduardo, the surgeon, called me a few days later to ask about my progress. I reported that I had needed little of the pain medication he prescribed and had even been able to work on this book for a half-day on the day following the extraction.

He asked what the book was about. I told him, "miracles, signs and wonders." That quickly ended the conversation.

Three days later Eduardo examined me and pronounced me in good shape. Then he asked, "Do you really see miracles, signs and wonders?"

"Yes. On a regular basis," I replied.

"You mean you actually see people get better in front of your eyes?"

"Yes."

"Tell me about one of your favorites so I have some idea what you are talking about."

I related the testimony of a child healed in an unusual way. Then I launched into an account about Drucilla. Eduardo was also suffering from sinus problems that day. His head was full and his speech was impacted. I wanted to tell him the testimony of Jesus most directly related to his problem.

I then asked Eduardo, "Do you want to see whether God will take care of that sinus stuff?"

He said, "Only say the word" and started moving away from us.

Nancy and I encouraged him to sit down while we prayed for him. He seemed reluctant to have us pray for him with his assistant in the room but we didn't ask her to leave.

After a short prayer, I instructed him, "Check it out." He began breathing deeply through his nose. With each breath we could all hear his head clear up.

Finally, he looked at his assistant and said, "Can you hear that?"

As we left that day, Eduardo was regaling the front office staff about what had happened to him in the exam room. Nancy and I got in the car, looked at one another and said, "He did it again." Both of us were in tears. God is so good. The testimony of Jesus is so powerful in releasing God's power.

One week later the phone rang during dinner. It was Eduardo. He just wanted us to know that he had been checking each day for the entire week to see if his symptoms would return. They did not!

A Life and Death Situation

We learned that Myrna was in the hospital with pneumonia on a Friday. Myrna is an older woman who suffered from pulmonary hypertension for many years as well as many other health problems. She had a long-standing relationship with her pulmonary doctor.

Before we left Granbury for the hospital in Fort Worth, we learned that Myrna was in intensive care. The next twenty-four hours were expected to either see her turn the corner toward recovery or death. She had been placed on life support. The family was gathering.

When we arrived in Fort Worth but were not yet at the hospital we learned that Myrna's heart had taken a turn for the worse and her kidneys were shutting down. Her prognosis was bleak.

At the hospital we told her husband, Pal, that we were going to go into ICU and pray for Myrna, if that was alright. I asked him what he believed God was doing in this situation. Was He calling her home to heaven or was she going home to Granbury? He said, "I certainly hope He's bringing her home to Granbury."

"Is that what Myrna wants," I asked.

"Yes."

"Have you asked her that specifically," I asked.

"Yes."

"Then that is what we will ask for."

Lynda (remember her), Nancy and I made our way into ICU. The women who were in the room left pretty quickly. The nurse completed one task and was out of the room.

Myrna looked nearly dead to me. She had tubes and stuff seemingly everywhere. She had strange things attached to her nose, mouth and face. She did not seem to be responsive to any outside stimulus.

Lynda told her, "Jeff and Nancy are here. We are going to pray for you."

I said, "Myrna, Pal tells me that you want to go home to Granbury. Is that right?"

Her only response was to nod her head almost imperceptively. Lynda was on her right side holding her right hand. Nancy was on her left side holding her left hand. I was at her feet.

We offered a short prayer. During the prayer, Myrna squeezed Nancy's hand several times, her breathing became much quicker, her eyelids fluttered and her body got hot. As we were nearing the end of our prayers, Myrna opened her eyes. It seemed to each of us she was much more aware of her circumstances.

Before we left, we changed positions so that I ended up with my hands on her head and Nancy had her hands on her chest. We offered a second short prayer. Once again her body was hot.

We retreated to the waiting room. I reported to Pal that we had seen God heal many, many people and I believed, based upon the physical sensations we felt during the prayer, that God was healing Myrna.

Myrna started a miraculous recovery. Within a couple days her doctor discussed transfer to a rehab facility. He said, "We have seen something truly amazing happen here. I could give Pal no hope. I did not think I would ever have the privilege of speaking with you again."

Myrna was transferred from ICU to a rehab facility. Her doctor informed her he expected a long, hard road to recovery.

The Monday following that transfer, Myrna's daughter asked me to do some legal work for Myrna and Pal. I spent the morning reviewing documentation and then went to Fort Worth to meet with Myrna. She was in ICU in the rehab hospital.

We walked into her room to find her sitting up in bed, hair combed, color in her face and delighted to see us. I asked, "Well, Myrna, how are you."

"Great!" she replied.

She told us, "My doctor told me with tears in his eyes that he did not expect to have the privilege of talking with me again. He told me he could not give Pal any hope. Now look at me."

"You look better than I have ever seen you," I said.

In order to do my work for Myrna she felt I needed to know some history of the situation. She talked quickly, accurately and forcefully to Nancy and me for the next ninety minutes. If she was having lung problems, they were not apparent to us.

When we saw Myrna the following day she had been moved out of ICU into a "normal" rehab room. She again was full of energy and looked better than we had ever seen her.

Each time we visited Myrna we were rendered nearly speechless by the enormity of what God had done. Myrna was telling everyone that God had healed her. We agreed!

Myrna walked out of rehab and went home twenty-eight days after the first prayers. Something amazing had indeed happened.

God Was Too Big.

Andrea is from Oklahoma. Her sister attends our church. She visited our church on her sister's birthday as a surprise to her sister.

As Andrea made her way down the aisle past us I noticed that she had an orthopedic boot on her left leg and foot, a back brace and was using a walker. She sat about four rows ahead of us on the aisle.

I immediately left my seat and made my way to her side as the praise team continued to worship. I quickly learned that she had fallen and was in sad shape. I told her, "If you are not healed by the end of the service, give us a chance to pray for you. You are not going to need that walker any longer." As I looked at her face it was obvious she was crying from the pain of walking down the aisle to her seat.

Following the service, several people who pray for others with us at that church gathered around Andrea. She reported that her back brace was because of recent surgery she had to remove metal rods which were previously implanted in her spine for support and a fusion of vertebrae. She had fallen and broken the metal rods. Her surgery was to remove the rods. She was wearing the back brace for support. She was not supposed to drive herself.

I asked about her orthopedic boot. She explained that nineteen months before she had sustained a second degree sprain to her left ankle. She had worn the boot since then. Her ankle was not improving and her left calf was atrophying at an alarming rate. The next step, according to her doctors, was pain management. They offered her no hope for treatment to fix her leg/ankle.

She also explained that she had the walker because she had balance issues from the left leg problems and the back surgery.

All of us gathered around her seated in her aisle seat. After a short prayer, I asked her to check it out.

"What do you mean?" she asked.

"Do something you couldn't do without pain and see what happens."

Andrea bent over in her seat reaching toward her left foot and began crying. I thought she was crying because of the pain of bending down toward her foot. I asked, "What's wrong?"

She looked first at me, then at Nancy and then back at me. She had a shocked look on her face. She obviously was having trouble accepting something that was happening to her.

She said, "I can't do this."

I said, "It seems that you are doing this."

She said, "It took me forty-five minutes to get this boot on this morning because of the pain in my back and my left leg and foot. Now, nothing hurts."

I asked, "Can you wiggle any part of your foot in that boot?"

She removed a Velcro-connected piece of the boot that covered her toes. She began to wiggle his big toe, all-the-while exclaiming that she couldn't do that. Then she began wiggling all of her toes. Between "wigglings," she would look at Nancy and then at me with that bewildered look on her face, seeming to inquire "What in the world is going on here."

Nancy said, "Let's take that boot completely off." Nancy helped her out of the boot.

Andrea than worked her ankle around and around in circles, reporting no pain. She repeatedly told us she couldn't do this. She then explained to Nancy that her left foot was extremely tender. She could tolerate no more than a sheet on the foot at night. It was extremely painful to have anyone or anything touch her foot. She then said, "Will you touch it so we can check it out."

Nancy grabbed her foot and squeezed and wiggled that foot in every direction. Andrea reported no pain.

By now, Andrea's extended family had gathered around her, waiting to go to lunch for her sister's birthday. Her niece was walking up and down the aisles holding up the orthopedic boot. Her brother-in-law was holding up her walker for all to see. He repeatedly told everyone there, "She hasn't been able to walk on that foot for nineteen months."

Andrea stood up to see about her balance and pain level. She continued the "deer in the headlights" looks at Nancy and me. She reported, "Nothing hurts."

I asked her to walk down our slanted aisle to see if walking was painful. She walked to the front and returned to our position to report no pain.

I told her that during the day she may be prompted to remove her back brace.

She told me, "This is great because I will not need pain pills anymore. That's good because there is a guy who lives in my house who steals my pain pills. This will put an end to that."

We learned from those gathered there the person was her daughter's boyfriend.

Andrea looked at a woman standing nearby with cute white shoes. She said, "I want a pair of shoes like that. I haven't worn a pair of shoes in nearly two years."

On the following Wednesday, Andrea's sister reported that Andrea had experiencef no further pain during the day. Mid-afternoon she had removed her back brace. She borrowed a pair of shoes from her sister and drove herself home to Oklahoma.

When she arrived home, it was obvious to her husband that she had experienced something rather important. He reported to her that their daughter's boyfriend, the one who was stealing the pain pills, had moved out while she was in Texas.

Andrea and her entire extended family were completely overwhelmed by God's goodness and power. Andrea's history had been changed in a moment.

When Nancy and I drove home, we struggled with the enormity of what we had just witnessed. Andrea had received a complete overhaul of her physical body, her mind and emotions and her living conditions had changed substantially for the better. Neither of us had been prepared for something on this scale.

I told Nancy that this was too huge. I said, "God is so powerful, so awesome, that it is scaring me. I cannot relate to a God who is so big. I need to get into the Gospels again and re-connect with Jesus to get over this fear and awe." Fortunately, reading the Gospels again calmed my spirit. I was still in total awe of what God had done but He was my Father once again.

Skin Healed While We Watched

Janice came to our regular Sunday night meeting with a bandage on her right index finger. Her entire hand was swollen and sore. She reported she had an open sore on her finger which she felt had healed. She then spent some time pulling weeds with no gloves on. The result was that the weeds irritated the pre-existing sore. We asked her to take off the bandage so we could pray for her. When the bandage was off we saw an extremely red finger, seemingly full of infection, and a very puffy hand.

The Sunday night group couldn't wait to pray for her to see what God had in store. We asked God to heal the sore on her finger, remove any infection and eliminate the swelling. Various members of the group added short prayers while we watched her finger and hand.

While we watched, her finger changed color from bright red to a normal pink skin color. We were all very impressed with the speed of the apparent recovery.

While we were whooping it up about the change in her finger, someone noticed that all of the swelling had gone out of her hand. It was a glorious time for this group. We had a lot of experience by then with orthopedic type problems immediately healed with no pain remaining. We had not dealt with a skin condition or an infection where we could watch the progress of the healing.

When God healed Janice's hand and finger, the entire group recognized a new high-water mark. After that time, we have come to expect to see immediate change. It is always stunning.

Perhaps the most stunning "immediate" change involved Beverly, the massage therapist friend of Art and Ginny. Ginny called and asked if they could bring Beverly to our house for prayer. She had a severe rash on both her hands that looked like psoriasis or a severe case of diaper rash. She was in such pain that the next stop was the hospital to handle the pain. We left the office immediately and met them at the house.

Beverly arrived with Art and Ginny. We looked at her hands and arms and understood immediately why she had such pain. The "rash" was so severe between the fingers on her right hand there were open, bleeding sores. The rest of her hands and both arms up to the elbow were just raw.

We sat her down while the four of us gathered around to pray. While we were praying I felt God's presence very strongly. I turned to Nancy and said, "Check your hands."

Usually when I feel electric Nancy has gold dust manifesting on her hands. She saw the gold dust on her hands and asked Beverly, "Do you know about gold dust?"

"No."

Nancy explained, "This is just a manifestation of God's presence. When I get this manifestation, it means God's power is also here. He doesn't leave home without it. And look, you have it all over your hands."

Sure enough, Beverly's hands were covered with gold dust. Art and Ginny both checked their hands and found gold dust there, too.

Nancy said, "Let's just rub this gold dust all over your hands and wrists and see what happens."

As we watched, over a period of about one hour, the gold dust on Beverly's hands spread progressively up her arms. As the gold dust spread, the redness was replaced by pink, healthy skin. At the end of the hour, Beverly reported no pain. We could see that the skin condition, whatever it had been, was gone.

When Beverly arrived home, her mother asked her, "What's that sparkly stuff all over your arms?"

The next day, Beverly used a cleanser in her office which she used to wash between clients. The red rash returned along with the pain. It was obvious she was experiencing an allergic reaction to the cleanser.

Beverly was confident that she could pray for her own healing. While she prayed, she once again experienced the gold dust. Once again, God healed the rash and removed the pain. The gold dust was obvious enough to see that she sent a picture from her cell phone which clearly showed the sparkles.

We know that God heals. We don't only believe it, we know it. We don't know how He will do it, when it will manifest, or what the final result will look like, but we know He heals.

CHAPTER TWELVE

Co-Laboring With God

I n all things, God is in charge and we are not. That is really
good news!

We participate in miracles, signs and wonders as a fellow
worker with God. Make no mistake; He always has the laboring
oar. The concept of *"God's fellow workers"* or *"workers together with
God"* (2 Corinthians 6:1) contains an important relational truth.
God is the worker, we are the fellow workers. We work together
with God. He doesn't work together with us.

Nancy and I began to participate in miracles, signs and
wonders when we stopped asking God to bless what we were
doing. We don't ask God to **help us** to accomplish our agenda.
Rather, we seek to determine what God is already blessing and
participate in that. It is His agenda, not ours.

Jesus does not come to us to receive His rest. We come to
Jesus to receive our rest. He does not take our yoke upon Him.
We take His yoke upon us. When we remember who is in charge
we are properly yoked.

> *"Take my yoke upon you and learn from me, for I am
> gentle and humble in heart, and you will find rest*

for your souls. For my yoke is easy and my burden is light." (Matthew 11:29-30)

Now, that's the way I want to work. What could be better than to be coupled with a much stronger partner who is both gentle and humble and who will let me rest? If I am going to be yoked, I need that yoke to be easy.

A Matter of Positioning

God is so far ahead of us it is staggering. The occurrences we find so convenient and amazing God has had planned for eons. The set-up for the miraculous of tomorrow was prepared long ago. He is the one who brings both parties to the table, the prayer and the one receiving prayer. He brings those parties together at just the right time for Him to pour out His compassion on His people.

God is an expert at *positioning* us so that we may participate in His miraculous interventions in history. Consider the Aramean siege of the nation of Israel in the walled city of Samaria. Let's identify the players.

The Government.

Joram, a son of Ahab, became king of Israel in the northern kingdom, which consisted of ten tribes. Joram's capitol city was the walled city of Samaria. He got rid of the stone of Baal which Ahab had made but he clung to the sins of Jeroboam.

The Church.

Elisha was a significant prophet. He had no use for Joram whatsoever. (2 Kings 3:14) Elisha had a prior history of participating in miracles, including raising the Shunnamite's son from the dead (2 Kings 4:31-36) and healing Naaman of leprosy. (2 Kings 5:1-15)

The Enemy.

Naaman was the commander of the Aramean army. He was healed of his leprosy when he reluctantly followed Elisha's instructions to dip himself in the Jordan seven times.

Ben Haddad was the king of Aram. He had continuing controversies with Joram and the nation of Israel. He had previously sent some of his army to capture Elisha in an attempt which failed completely.

God was teaching Israel that its security came from Him alone, not from Joram and not from Elisha. In the midst of those circumstances, Ben Haddad sent his entire army, commanded by Naaman, to lay siege to the walled city of Samaria.

The siege caused a severe famine within the city. The famine was so bad that two women made a pact to kill and eat their babies. After the first baby was eaten, the second mother reneged and hid her child.

Joram received the complaint of the second woman while he was walking the walls of the city. His immediate response was anger toward Elisha, apparently believing this bad fortune for the nation of Israel was part of the on-going battle between the two.

In the midst of the famine and hidden baby problem, Elisha prophesied:

> *"Hear the word of the LORD. This is what the LORD says: About this time tomorrow, a seah of flour will sell for a shekel and two seahs of barley for a shekel at the gate of Samaria."* (2 Kings 7:1)

This prophecy was met with complete skepticism.

Sitting outside the walled city of Samaria were four lepers. Because of their leprosy, they were unclean and completely unwelcome in the city. Since they were part of the besieged nation of Israel, they had no food either.

The same day that Elisha prophesied the coming abundance of food, the lepers had an interesting conversation.

> *"Why sit we here until we die? If we say, 'We will enter into the city,' then the famine is in the city, and we shall die there; and if we sit still here, we die also. Now therefore come, and let us fall unto the host of the Syrians; if they save us alive, we shall live; and if they kill us, we shall but die."*
> (2 Kings 7:3-4 KJV)

"Why sit we here until we die?" This is a critical question for all believers. Once I am saved, what am I to do? Is there a purpose for me or do I just sit here until I die?

The lepers decided on that occasion, not a day before or day later, to go to the enemy's camp. While they were on the way, and totally unbeknownst to them, God performed a miracle that rescued the entire nation of Israel.

> *"The Lord . . . caused the Arameans to hear the sound of chariots and horses and a great army, so that they said to one another, "Look, the king of Israel has hired the Hittite and Egyptian kings to attack us!" So they got up and fled in the dusk and abandoned their tents and their horses and donkeys. They left the camp as it was and ran for their lives."*
> (2 Kings 7:6-7)

The food and provisions which the army left behind saved the lives of the entire nation of Israel.

Consider:

o   Who performed the miracle?
o   Who participated in the miracle?
o   What part did each play?
o   Who got the glory?

God alone caused the Aramean army to hear chariots and horses and a great army. They didn't hear the lepers approaching and run off in fear. They were terrified by what God caused them to hear.

Neither the lepers nor any of the residents of the walled city of Samaria heard those chariots and horses. The reason is simple— the army did not exist in the physical realm!

The church didn't do it.

Elisha cannot be credited for the miracle. Elisha did nothing except repeat what he heard God saying. He did absolutely nothing to bring this result to pass. He did not call the nation of Israel to prayer or take any action.

The government didn't do it.

Joram cannot be credited for the miracle. Joram did nothing except threaten to kill Elisha. He did not even call out to God for help.

The enemy didn't do it.

Naaman cannot be credited for the miracle. Naaman stood in awe of the God of Israel because he had experienced the power of

God in his healing from leprosy. Naaman knew that his army was laying siege to a nation that was blessed by God Himself. When Naaman and his soldiers heard the sounds, he believed that other nation's armies were coming. The army ran in fear.

The lepers didn't do it.

The lepers cannot be credited for the miracle. The enemy did not depart in fear of the approaching lepers. The enemy was terrified by sounds of the heavenly host which only they could hear.

The lepers' function in the miracle was to report the good news and share the bounty. God prompted the four lepers to get up at that very time. Had they not gone, when would the nation of Israel have learned that God was blessing them with abundance? All the lepers knew was they were walking for food or death. They did not intend to participate in a miracle.

God did not perform this miracle because of:

o   Elisha's actions as a prophet over a prolonged period;
o   Joram's actions as king of Israel; a desire to punish Naaman or Ben Haddad; any "righteousness" of the lepers; or anyone in the circumstance was good.

God performed this miracle for the same reason He performs them all. God performs miracles because He is good and He loves His people. He was not rewarding anyone for good actions. The people of Israel were killing and eating their children. The government was at odds with the church. Distrust and destructive behavior was rampant. They weren't good. He was.

No one knew God was acting.

Each of the participants in this event participated in a miracle without realizing it. No one realized God was performing a miraculous intervention in Israel's history and pouring out His compassion on His people while it was happening. The realization of the truth awaited a report from the unclean and unwelcome lepers of the blessings now available to God's people.

No one did anything more than be where God positioned them and report what he saw and heard. The religious followers of Elisha (and Elisha himself) were unable to deliver God's compassion to His people. The existing government, Joram and his army could do nothing other than permit the blessing to be received. Most likely, the ones who reported the blessing were still not permitted within the city because the leprosy persisted.

God did it all, from beginning to end. He intervened in the history of His people to demonstrate His compassion and His love. No one prayed to God to change His mind. God was not rewarding the faith of anyone involved in the circumstances.

Each of the lepers was a fellow worker with God. He didn't help them perform the miracle. The miracle was not a product of power He granted to them. Rather, He positioned them in a way to observe and report what He was doing.

Elisha was a fellow worker with God. God didn't help Elisha accomplish any result. Elisha was positioned in a way to speak God's word to the people so that when the miracle was discovered the following day all the glory would be given to God.

All the co-laboring followed God's plan, not man's plan. What could be easier than simply being in the right place, positioned by God, and doing what God prompts you to do when He prompts you to do it? Had the lepers jumped the gun, they likely would have been killed. Instead, God prompted them to take their halting steps in pursuit of His purposes.

The lepers were not experts in delivering God's compassion to His people. Yet, they were used mightily by God to accomplish His purposes.

Miraculous healings today are accomplished in exactly the same fashion. Someone may have a word of knowledge that God is going to heal a particular person or a particular condition. However, that knowledge does not enable the person in his own power to heal anyone. The person being healed may feel something and recognize the power of God is upon him, or he may not. The confirmation of many miraculous healings awaits a sensory perception of a change that cannot be explained in any way other than an act of God.

CHAPTER THIRTEEN
Persisting In Prayer

Jesus told his disciples the parable of the unjust judge *"to show them that they should always pray and not give up."* (Luke 18:1) After reciting the parable, Jesus said,

> *"And will not God bring about justice for his chosen ones, who cry out to him day and night? Will he keep putting them off? I tell you, he will see that they get justice, and quickly. However, when the Son of Man comes, will he find faith on the earth?"* (Luke 18:7-8)

In the realm of supernatural healing and delivery from torment, *justice* requires that Jesus receives what He bought and paid for. Since both healing and delivery from torment are in the atonement, they are *already established* in the kingdom. *Justice* in the kingdom requires that Jesus receive what He has already redeemed.

Jesus ends His explanation of the parable with a question. Will the Son of Man find faith on the earth upon his return? Jesus asked whether upon His return he would find people filled with and acting upon faith. Those who are filled with faith know that healing and delivery from torment are present day realities in the kingdom, waiting to be manifested in our bodies and souls. The price has been paid. The manifestation awaits our amen. (2 Corinthians 1:20) Any delay in the manifestation does not negate what has already been established.

Just as a change in destination is not manifested until we confess the "word of faith," physical healing or delivery from torment may not yet be manifested, but each is equally available. Jesus wanted to know whether upon His return He would find His people exercising their faith in the unseen. *"Now faith is being sure of what we hope for and certain of what we do not see."* (Hebrews 11:1) We should be as sure of our physical healing and delivery from torment as we are sure of our change in destination.

When a believer utters the "word of faith," Jesus does not then decide whether He will change the believer's destination. That change is already in place.

In the exact same fashion, when there is a prayer for healing or delivery from torment, Jesus does not then decide whether the Father is both willing and able to heal or deliver from torment. "We do not persist in prayer in order to change God's mind." (Bill Johnson, *Healing, Our Neglected Birthright*) Our current prayers have no ability to change or add to what Jesus accomplished on His way to the cross. The price has been paid. By His stripes, we are healed. (Isaiah 53:5)

Matters which are already established in the kingdom do not necessarily manifest themselves in our lives. Jesus came to His own people. They did not receive Him. *"Yet to all who received him, to those who believed in his name, he gave the right to become children of God—children born not of natural descent, nor of human decision or a husband's will, but born of God."* John 1:12-13) All sins of all people have been forgiven by Jesus' death and resurrection.

That forgiveness is already available but must be received to effect a change. God gave us, through Jesus' death and resurrection, the *right* to become His children. When I exercised that right, Jesus did not come again to die for the forgiveness of my sins. It was already done.

When we pray for divine healing or delivery from torment, we are asking for something that is already done. We are simply asking for a manifestation of the truth already established in the kingdom.

God's response to prayer is not conditioned upon our current behavior. Rather, His response depends entirely upon His great mercy. God does not wait for us to be good to manifest His goodness.

Daniel prayed for Jerusalem and God's people, saying,

> *"We do not make requests of you because we are righteous, but because of your great mercy."* (Daniel 9:18)

While Daniel was still speaking and praying, Gabriel appeared and said,

> *"Daniel, I have now come to give you insight and understanding. As soon as you began to pray, an answer was given, which I have come to tell you, for you are highly esteemed."* (Daniel 9:22-23)

God heard Daniel's prayers *as soon as he began to pray.* The response to that prayer was delivered through Gabriel immediately. Healing is sometimes like that. In many instances, complete and total healing manifests itself as soon as we begin to pray. Sometimes we discern healing even before the prayer begins.

It is not unusual for those who are praying to be healed while they are praying for someone else. At the conclusion of the prayer, the persons praying discover they have likewise received healing or delivery from torment without any request by anyone at the time. It is a collateral blessing.

Other times, healing manifests at a later time. Until the manifestation comes, we are to be persistent in prayer. God is neither bored nor tired of hearing from us.

Daniel experienced a delayed response to his prayer also. Daniel received a revelation which he did not understand. He sought an explanation from God. Daniel mourned for three weeks waiting for the explanation. After three weeks, Gabriel appeared to Daniel again. Gabriel explained,

> "Do not be afraid, Daniel. Since the first day that you set your mind to gain understanding and to humble yourself before your God, your words were heard, and I have come in response to them. But the prince of the Persian kingdom resisted me twenty-one days. Then Michael, one of the chief princes, came to help me, because I was detained there with the king of Persia." (Daniel 10:12-13)

Just as in the prior encounter with Gabriel, Daniel was assured that God heard his prayers on "the first day [he] set [his] mind to gain understanding." Just as in the prior encounter, God sent Gabriel immediately. However, Gabriel encountered resistance in the spirit realm. Michael was then dispatched to assist Gabriel to escape from his encounter with the liar. The result was a delay from the request until the delivery of the requested understanding. The understanding had already been given in the kingdom but had not yet manifested itself to Daniel because of resistance in the spirit realm.

Any understanding of a reason for a delay between the prayer for healing and the manifestation is elusive. The two experiences Daniel had are illustrative of the fact that sometimes the manifestation is quick and complete and other times the manifestation awaits further developments.

God was not waiting on Daniel to do anything more than ask. The day he asked for understanding, Gabriel was dispatched. The delay was not on God's end and not necessarily on Daniel's end. All we really are told is that there was spiritual resistance by the liar which held up the manifestation for a season. When God's compassion is delivered it is an act of war in the liar's realm.

Keep On Asking

The parable of the persistent neighbor instructs us to keep on asking. In explaining that parable, Jesus said,

> *"So I say to you: Ask and it will be given to you; seek and you will find; knock and the door will be opened to you. For everyone who asks receives; he who seeks finds; and to him who knocks, the door will be opened."* (Luke 11:9-10; Matthew 7:7-8)

The Greek grammar in this passage uses the present imperative and present participles. In this context, the proper translation is ask—and *keep on asking*; seek—and *keep on seeking*; knock—and *keep on knocking*. Do not assume that a delay between your asking and your receiving implies a withholding of God's favor. We are to persist in our prayers.

Delay and My Shoulder

In 1963 I started having recurrent sublaxations of my left shoulder while playing high school football. In high school there was no pain, just a weird sensation as my shoulder joint dislocated and then went back into place spontaneously.

At West Point in 1966 I again had problems with sublaxations while playing football. This time the sliding of the bones in the joint as the shoulder dislocated and spontaneously repositioned was exquisitely painful. The sublaxations were not limited to the football field but occurred in the classroom and in my bed at night. In February, 1967, I had my first surgery to "tighten up" my shoulder. The surgeon told me not to do work "over head" following that surgery.

By 1977 I was in trouble again with that same shoulder. Lifting my children over my head and other stupid acts had brought the sublaxations back. The pain was quite amazing. In late spring, 1977, I had my second surgery to not only tighten up the joint but to cut off a piece of bone with my biceps tendon attached and reposition it across the shoulder joint with a screw. I was told my next surgery, if I wasn't careful, would be an artificial shoulder. I thought the surgeon was joking.

In March, 1996, Dr. Charles A. Rockwood performed a total shoulder replacement surgery on that left shoulder. He explained to me that due to all the scar tissue from the prior surgeries there was a chance I would experience nerve damage during this procedure.

I did, indeed, experience nerve damage during the surgery. The result was that I was no longer able to lift my left arm to permit me to put my left hand on top of my head. There was no mechanical blockage to prevent lifting my arm. Rather, the problem was one of strength. The deltoid muscle which primarily lifts the arm at the shoulder completely atrophied. I could lift my left arm with my right arm but the left one simply had no strength for that motion.

As a result of the atrophy, I looked like an Auschwitz survivor on my left side from the center of my chest through the upper margin of my biceps and triceps muscles in my left arm. All that was visible was skin and bone.

Nonetheless, I was thrilled with my shoulder replacement. The bone-on-bone grinding was gone. What a relief. I was basically pain free. The limitations in my range of motion and my inability to put my hand on top of my head did not significantly interfere with my every-day activities.

There were many times after 1977 when I have prayed for a healing of my shoulder. I vividly recall the disappointment I felt when all of my friends began lifting their hands in prayer and praise during worship services. I tried but was unable to make my left arm perform satisfactorily to me. When I was watching a performance by Terry Talbot in 1978 I prayed for an increase in my range of motion so that I could raise both hands above my head without restriction. Although I tried, I just didn't have the ability to raise my left arm as high as I thought it should go.

Periodically between 1996 and 2008 I would pray for a return of my muscles and the ability to lift my left arm above what little I could muster with the remaining muscles. I would then try to get that arm going to no avail.

I have already related the difference between the prayers for Nancy's hands and the prayers for my shoulder. Nancy's hands were healed. I noticed no difference in my shoulder. I did my best to fight through the disappointment of not being healed in my shoulder by rejoicing in the healing of Nancy's hands.

By 2010, we had "progressed" in the group who met in our home to the point where we were experiencing significant, miraculous healings on a regular basis. Sunday night at our house was a very exciting time. We were seeing miracles through the week in restaurants and places of business. We were seeing miracles at our home. We even saw some miracles at church.

In early August, 2010, I asked for prayer to heal my shoulder on a Sunday night. I was reluctant to ask for fear that, just as the many times prior, nothing would happen. But, I asked nonetheless. I am not certain I believed anything would happen but I was both hopeful and greedy. I wanted to experience the healing we were seeing on a regular basis one more time.

After the short prayer for my shoulder, I could discern no immediate change in my shoulder after the prayer. I did my best to lift my arm but did not feel there was any improvement in my ability.

The following week, we prayed again. However, the man who had his hand on my shoulder told me, "Jeff, there is more stuff there than last week." I still could not lift my arm any higher. I was battling with myself to continue asking for prayer. My desire was to ask B and keep on asking. However, the liar sat on my shoulder telling me that God wasn't going to heal this one.

Eighteen days after the first prayer for my shoulder, I noticed substantially improved range of motion while in the swimming pool. Since 1996 the only swimming stoke I could perform was the breast stroke. It was quite abbreviated because I couldn't get my left arm to go very far toward my side. I started doing the breast stroke in the pool that day and noticed that I could make a slightly more complete stroke. I stood in the water and moved my arm forward and backward around my body with significantly more range of motion than I had previously. I didn't say anything to Nancy at that time.

That evening I was lying on the couch watching TV. I turned to Nancy to explain to her that I had experienced the improved range of motion while we were in the pool. In making the explanation, I found myself scratching the top of my head with my left hand. I said, "I can't do this, can I?"

Nancy said, "You haven't been able to do that since I have known you."

My motion in putting my hand on top of my head was halting and nearly spastic, but it got the job done.

When I stood up to show Nancy the improved range of motion, I found I could get my left arm behind me far enough to meet the right one. What a change.

My movement putting my hand on top of my head smoothed over time. It seemed like God had healed the nerve damage and my muscles were slowly re-learning the proper function.

Through the next several weeks, I stretched aggressively to stretch out the muscles which had contracted significantly, limiting my range of motion. As those muscles relaxed and stretched, I had more and more range of motion. The more I put my hand on top of my head, the better coordinated I was and the less effort it took.

In November, we went to Sojourn Church in Carrolton to see Bill Johnson again. During the opening worship on Friday night, I felt intense pain in the area where my lateral deltoid muscle had been. When I looked at my arm I noticed that my arm completely filled the sleeve of my shirt. My shoulder had been so atrophied that I had shoulder pads added to my suits so the deficit was not as noticeable. I turned to Nancy and said, "My arm is killing me. I think it is growing."

She looked at me with that "you must be joking" look. Then she looked at my shirt sleeve. Her eyes widened as she said, "I think you are right."

I now have a greatly restored deltoid muscle and the muscles on the left side of my chest are larger than on the right side.

Jeffrey B. Thompson

God restored the nerve in August and then grew the muscles in November. I know for certain I didn't do it.

I cannot explain how, why or when the nerves to my shoulder muscles were healed. I have related what I observed but I had no sense of healing at the time. I can't say whether the healing started the first day, the next week or in the pool.

I can, however, report *Who* did it—and it wasn't me or my friends who prayed for me. Only God can grow muscles during a worship service.

I am confident that God heard my prayers and the prayers of others from the beginning. I am confident that He never gave up on me or my condition. I am confident that my healing continues to manifest to this day and will do so in the future.

I don't know whether battles were being waged in the spirit realm over the healing God sent my way. I can only report that from 1996 to 2010 I was unable to put my left hand on the top of my head without using my other hand to lift it—and now I can.

Do not be discouraged if there is not an immediate manifestation of healing or delivery from torment. Ask—and keep on asking. Seek—and keep on seeking. Knock—and keep on knocking.

I have been impressed for the last three years to tell people who have conditions that have lasted for a long time that God is not done with them. I believe the passage of time is not an indicator that God has given up on the condition. I do not believe the passage of time indicates that God is trying to teach us a lesson before healing us.

I didn't learn any lesson that opened the door to God healing my shoulder. Jesus bought and paid for my shoulder healing on His way to the cross. That healing is now manifesting itself in my body.

We have prayed for many others who have had long standing conditions. Our experience is that:

o   those people whose legs have grown out to be even with the other leg while we watched have had a short leg for quite a while but have it no longer;

o   Mark had pain in his knee for more than fifteen years but has it no longer;

o   Claude had an ankle which was essentially fused for more than seven years but has it no longer; the people who have had tingling and burning pain in their lower legs and feet have been in that condition for many years but they have it no longer;

o   Mary, who had scoliosis in her back that caused one leg to manifest as shorter than the other and caused her back pain had been that way for many years but she has it no longer; and many, many people who have been freed from torment were tormented for quite a while but are tormented no longer.

It is a continual fight to not let disappointment lead to abandonment of hope. I am convinced that God is never satisfied when one of His children is oppressed by the devil. He has never stopped acting on behalf of His children.

Expect a miracle at any moment, even when many moments have already passed. He's not done!

CHAPTER FOURTEEN
The Benefits of a Renewed Mind

Nancy and I have spent innumerable hours discussing what has happened in our lives. How is that we are now experiencing God's goodness and power on a regular basis? What changed in our circumstances that produced this result? We needed to know the answer to these questions for two reasons. First, we didn't want to do anything that might take us back to where we had been. Second, we wanted to be able to explain to others what happened to us so that it could happen to them.

The renewing of our mind changed our way of thinking, just as Jesus instructed. (Mark 1:15) With our renewed minds, we were better able to believe the good news and take Jesus at His word.

If I can keep the good news of the kingdom dominating my thoughts, I am continually encouraged. That encouragement brings with it a change in my behavior. I don't have time to pursue things outside the kingdom if I am constantly pursuing the things of the kingdom.

No New Tricks

The liar is basically a one-trick pony. He does not want my allegiance. He wants me to turn my back on God. If he can get me distracted from God's purposes, it will grieve God's heart.

A one-trick pony has a limited repertoire but is very good at its one trick. Having seen the trick, the show is over. The liar uses the same old approach to spear us. That spear is two pronged, but only one spear.

The liar exposed both prongs of his spear in dealing with the first Adam (Genesis 3) and the second Adam (Luke 4:3; Luke 4:9). In the garden, the liar invited Adam to question the word of God. In the temptations of Jesus, the liar invited Him to question whether He was, indeed, the Son of God.

This one-trick pony will aim the same spear at us. We should be prepared to resist every invitation to:

o   question God's word; or
o   question our relationship to God.

A renewed mind can more easily take Jesus at His word. When Jesus promises something, it is settled. Those promises are all true Because He Said So.

A renewed mind can more easily remember our status as a new creation in the kingdom. A renewed mind will not waste time trying to gain or acquire a relationship to God that Jesus already purchased. We become acceptable to God by having faith in Jesus as our Lord and believing that God raised Him from the dead. We are acceptable Because He Said So.

As a matter of discipline, Nancy and I no longer permit our experience to cause us to question the truth of what Jesus has said. We are experiencing miracles, signs and wonders on an unprecedented level (for us). We do not permit the occasions when it *appears that nothing happens* when we pray to discourage us.

You will experience miracles, signs and wonders that will astonish you when your renewed mind takes Jesus at His word and believes:

o God is able to do exceedingly, abundantly above all that we can ask or imagine, according to His power that is at work within us. (Ephesians 3:20)

o All sin, sickness and torment are from the devil.

o Jesus is the exact representation of the Father. (Hebrews 1:3)

o Jesus was made manifest to destroy the works of the devil. (1 John 3:8)

o Jesus is the same, yesterday, today and forever. (Hebrews 3:8)

o The testimony of Jesus is the spirit of prophecy. (Revelation 19:10)

o God anointed Jesus of Nazareth with the Holy Spirit and with power and He went around doing good, healing all who were oppressed by the devil, because God was with Him. (Acts 10:38)

o By Himself, Jesus could no nothing. Rather, He only did what He saw the Father doing (John 5:19) and only said what He heard the Father saying. (John 8:28; John 12:50)

o Jesus sends us as the Father sent Him. (John 20:21)

o We receive power from on high through Baptism in the Holy Spirit. (Luke 24:49; Acts 1:4-8)

o Anyone who has faith in Jesus will do the things He did, and greater things also. (John 14:12) o   Whoever hears Jesus' word and believes the one who sent Him has eternal life and will not be condemned; he has crossed over from death to life. (John 5:24)

o   The Law and the Prophets were until John. Since then the good news of the kingdom is being preached. (Luke 16:16)

Your renewed mind will readily embrace that, in the kingdom:

o   I am a new creation (2 Corinthians 5:17);

o   I am the righteousness of God (2 Corinthians 5:21);

o   God is not counting my sins against me (2 Corinthians 5:19) and remembers my sins no more (Hebrews 8:12);

o   I am perfect while I am being made holy (Hebrews 10:14);

o   The kingdom of God is not primarily concerned with behavior but rather is righteousness, peace and joy in the Holy Spirit (Romans 14:17); and

o   I have been set free from the power of sin (Romans 6:14-18; Hebrews 9:15).

About the Author

Jeffrey B. Thompson is a lawyer with a general law practice in Granbury, about twenty five miles southwest of Fort Worth, Texas. He and his wife, Nancy, relocated to Granbury in 2006 after spending more than thirty years as a trial lawyer in complex civil litigation for clients in or connected to El Paso.

While in El Paso, Jeff was an associate pastor for five years at the House of Cornelius and a member of the board of directors there for fifteen years. The House of Cornelius was a non-denominational Christian home for both children and families founded and directed by Gilberto ("Buddy") Baca and his wife, Georgia.

Beginning in 2008, Jeff and Nancy began to routinely witness God's miraculous intervention in the lives of His people. They have repeatedly witnessed history being changed before their eyes. They have come to know that physical, mental and emotional healing is part of Jesus' DNA. They now expect nothing different when they pray with others.

Together they have presented the material discussed in Because He Said So in Granbury and Benbrook for the last three years. They emphasize that miracles, signs and wonders should manifest in the lives of all believers when they pray using the concepts addressed in this book. The class members' experiences have proved them right time and again.

Jeff and Nancy are available to address your church or conduct a series of classes to equip a group of believers in your church who are willing to participate with God in delivering His compassion to His people. No experts are required.

Website: www.becausehesaidso.com

Email: jbt@becausehesaidso.com

Address: Jeffrey B. Thompson
             1030 E. Hwy 377
             Suite 110-370
             Granbury, Texas 76048

Telephone: 817-573-5509